# LIFE INSURANCE
# WEALTH CODE

## UNLOCKING TAX-FREE FINANCIAL ABUNDANCE

## BENJAMIN WATERFORD

# ACKNOWLEDGMENTS

Writing a book is not a solitary endeavor; it is the result of countless hours of hard work, collaboration, and the support of many people. I am very grateful to everyone who contributed to the creation of this book, "Life Insurance Wealth Code: Unlocking Tax-free Financial Abundance." Your support and encouragement have been invaluable on this journey.

First and foremost, I want to express my deep gratitude to my family. To my spouse, for her unwavering support, patience, and understanding during the long hours I spent researching and writing. To my wonderful children, for their resilience and for allowing me the time to pursue this passion. Your love and support mean the world to me.

To my friends and colleagues in the financial industry, thank you for sharing your knowledge and insights over the years. Your expertise has been a wellspring of inspiration for this book.

My sincere appreciation goes out to the readers and reviewers who provided valuable feedback and helped refine the content. Your insights have undoubtedly enhanced the quality of this work.

I also extend my thanks to the professionals and experts in the field of life insurance and financial planning who generously shared their knowledge and experiences. Your contributions have added depth and credibility to the ideas presented in this book.

Finally, I would like to acknowledge the countless individuals who have entrusted me with their financial well-being and shared their stories with me. Your trust and confidence have motivated me to continuously seek ways to improve financial security and abundance for all.

To all of you, thank you for your unwavering support, encouragement, and inspiration. This book would not have been possible without each and every one of you. May the ideas within these pages serve as a source of empowerment and financial well-being for all who read them.

With heartfelt thanks,

Benjamin Waterford

# ABOUT THE AUTHOR

Benjamin Waterford is a seasoned financial advisor with over two decades of experience in the industry. His experience and dedication to helping individuals and families to achieve their financial goals has made him a respected authority in the field. Throughout his career, he has been a tireless advocate for sound financial planning. His perspective on utilizing life insurance as a cornerstone of financial well-being has helped countless people to secure there financial future and protect loved ones.

In this book, he is thrilled to share his in-depth knowledge and insights to guide readers towards a path of financial prosperity. In this book he demystifies the seemingly complex world of life insurance, providing readers with a clear road-map to harness the power of tax-free wealth accumulation.

This book is dedicated to those who possess the courage to dream, the determination to act, and the resilience to make the world as they want it. Your unwavering commitment to turning visions into reality, and your tireless efforts to create a better future, inspire us all.

May the knowledge and insights within these pages serve as tools to empower your journey and contribute to your mission of shaping a world that reflects your aspirations.

With deep admiration and gratitude,

Benjamin Waterford

# CONTENTS

# INTRODUCTION

Imagine you have a large lump sum of money or a sizable amount of extra income each month you want to invest for the future.

You consider the usual investments: Stocks, bonds, mutual funds, maybe real estate. You wonder if you should add a little more money to your 401(k) or IRA, but you hesitate. Those accounts make you wait many years before you can take your money out without paying a penalty.

You consider risk, returns and tax implications of your choices. This rules out savings bonds, high-turnover mutual funds, and whatever those Nigerian princes keep emailing you about.

You talk it over with your friends, relatives and the financial planner from your church. None of them provides clarity.

Then somebody you trust hands you this book, or maybe you find it on Amazon while searching for an e-book on smart investing. A few days later, you're convinced to put your money in an asset you had never considered.

Life insurance.

**Why you need this information**

If you're like most of the people I meet and counsel, you have one or more of the following financial concerns:

- You're struggling to find the sweet spot in your investment portfolio between maximizing your returns and minimizing your risk.
- You're concerned with having enough life insurance to protect your family.
- You wonder how you're going to help your children pay for college.
- You worry about having enough for retirement income, even if you're still decades away from retirement.
- You need a bigger emergency fund in the event of job loss or health concern.
- You're concerned about liquidity.
- Your estate plan is incomplete or nonexistent.
- You struggle to understand the complexity of financial and tax planning.
- You hate the thought of paying a large share of your income and investment returns in state and federal taxes.
- You don't have the stomach for high-risk investments, especially after hearing about people who invested with Bernie Madoff or Enron.

The two reasons I wrote this book are that:

1. I've heard these issues expressed so often by so many; and
2. I discovered an underutilized asset that addresses each one of these concerns.

Yep, life insurance.

## What you're going to accomplish

Specifically, I wrote this book to address the value and versatility of permanent cash value life insurance, which includes whole life and universal life.

Whole life and universal life insurance policies accumulate cash value over time. This cash value earns interest on a tax-deferred basis. This makes it a potent tool in wealth creation and preservation, going beyond its conventional role as just a safety net.

What's more, life insurance provides a way for policy owners to access this cash value on a tax-free basis. This provides a potential source of self-financing, emergency funds and regular income that can help you achieve tax-free financial abundance and retain more of your wealth.

You will also retain more of your wealth by avoiding investment losses that commonly occur when you invest in stocks, mutual funds, or real estate. Most permanent life insurance policies have a built-in floor that prevents any type of market-based loss. You may trade the potential for higher returns by using life insurance, but you also won't be settling for minuscule returns that many "safe" investments offer. Plus, your money will potentially accumulate faster when it's guaranteed to never decline in value.

Life insurance also has the added benefit of helping to secure the future of your family and/or business in the event you pass away. When it comes to permanent life insurance, you can guarantee that benefit for the remainder of your life provided you pay the required premiums. It can also benefit your family in the event you get seriously sick or injured by providing optional "living benefits."

Plus, when it comes time to shift your focus from wealth accumulation to wealth preservation, life insurance is the ideal financial tool to help you fund an estate plan that will ensure a smooth transfer of wealth to your heirs.

**What you're going to learn**

Some of the lessons this book emphasizes include:

- Debunking the myths of life insurance that often prevent people from considering it a wealth-building asset.
- Several examples of how life insurance can help you build tax-efficient wealth.
- How life insurance can help you navigate the uncertainties and complexities of the current economy.
- How the tax advantages on life insurance work.
- How cash value life insurance has provided famous entrepreneurs liquidity when they needed it and how it can do the same for you.

- How life insurance minimizes the various risks that occur with other types of investments.
- How to evaluate life insurance policies to make the right decision for your specific needs.
- Using advanced strategies with life insurance to enhance your overall financial plan.
- The ongoing tasks you should address over time to ensure your financial and estate plans continue to meet your needs.

One last thing. I realize life insurance may not be the most interesting topic to read about. I'm also aware that it's often full of jargon and numbers and can be confusing to understand.

I promise you won't have that problem with this book. I've intentionally made it short and to the point. There is no sales fluff and a minimal amount of insurance lingo, and what it does contain is clearly explained. The book provides clear, actionable steps and solutions you can implement in your own life.

I want you to get through this text as quickly as possible so that you can begin to adopt the principles I've covered and start growing your tax-efficient wealth.

And who knows? After you've finished, you may develop an appreciation for life insurance and find it as fascinating a topic as I have over the years.

Yep, life insurance.

# TAX-EFFICIENT WEALTH BUILDING: THE POTENTIAL OF LIFE INSURANCE

*"In this world, nothing is certain except death and taxes."*

— BENJAMIN FRANKLIN

W hile most Americans are familiar with this famous quote by one of the nation's founding fathers, few know the context in which Benjamin Franklin used it.

In November 1789, about six months before his death, Franklin wrote a letter to French scientist Jean-Baptiste Le Roy, a close friend. The letter's main purpose was to inquire about Le Roy's well-being. Franklin had not heard from his friend since the start of the French Revolution earlier that year.

Why did Franklin care about the well-being of a French scientist? He made friends in that country serving as an ambassador to France. In addition, his electricity experiments made him well-known in the scientific community.

(Turns out, Le Roy was ok. One can probably forgive his lack of correspondence with Franklin since he may have been distracted by the nationwide revolt going on around him. Also, this was many years before air travel and email made international communication more practical.)

After asking Le Roy about what was happening in France, Franklin took the opportunity to inform him of the great news that the U.S. Constitution had been ratified. This is where the famous line originated.

**"Our new Constitution is now established, everything seems to promise it will be durable; but, in this world, nothing is certain except death and taxes,"** Franklin wrote in French. The letter was translated in 1817 when Franklin's private papers were published.

Franklin had confidence the nation's new government could last generations. Yet he understood the world was filled with risks powerful enough to potentially topple the United States. This is something to keep in mind as you read the rest of this book; there is uncertainty everywhere.

At the same time, Franklin knew from experience that people could mitigate risk and not succumb to the uncertainties of life. This was possible through the power of insurance.

Franklin lived in Philadelphia in 1730 when a devastating fire in the Fishbourn's wharf destroyed stores and homes. In 1752, he and several other leading citizens founded the Philadelphia

Contributionship for the Insurance of Houses from Loss by Fire, modeled after a London firm.

Seven years later, Franklin helped form the country's first life insurance company, the Presbyterian Ministers' Fund.

More than 250 years later, life insurance is a financial tool that millions of Americans use to deal with both death and taxes.

## THE TRANSFORMATIVE POWER OF LIFE INSURANCE

In Franklin's day, life insurance was more rudimentary. It gave survivors the ability to financially carry on with life after a man's death, one that would typically leave families without any form of income.

Today, life insurance has transformative powers:

- It helps people build wealth over time, even while they're still alive.
- It can mitigate a number of financial risks, not just untimely death.
- It has the power to provide tax-free financial abundance.
- It helps create and preserve generational wealth against the risks of death and taxes — as well as debt and inflation.
- It has become one of the most versatile financial assets for families at all income levels.

## TACKLING 20 MYTHS ABOUT LIFE INSURANCE

Sound too good to be true?

If so, you may have heard and believed in one or more of the many myths about today's life insurance policies. These falsehoods have been perpetuated over time by so-called experts who either don't understand the evolution of life insurance or who have self-serving incentives to steer you away from life insurance as a financial asset.

So before I go into great detail about the powerful potential of life insurance, let's tackle those myths, shall we?

Here are my responses to the 20 most prolific distortions, inaccuracies and misconceptions about life insurance.

### Myths about buying and owning life insurance

**Myth #1: Life Insurance is a scam.** On the contrary, life insurance is one of the greatest risk management and financial management tools ever created.

- Policy death benefits help grieving families financially recover from the loss of a loved one.
- Life insurance helps people offset the costs of dying, such as funeral expenses and legal fees that arise when settling an estate.
- It helps families efficiently pass on their estate to their heirs.
- It helps preserve the financial legacy that people worked hard to build.

- It enables people to pass on generous gifts to grandchildren and favorite charities after their passing.
- Regular premium payments over time generate additional savings as well as produce a large lump sum that is passed on to the insured's surviving beneficiaries.
- Life insurance accomplishes all of this without the extra burden of paying taxes on the benefits it creates.

**Myth #2: Life Insurance is expensive**. In some ways buying life insurance is like purchasing a house or a car. You can overpay for it if you don't know what you're buying. It's possible to get talked into getting the top of the line option that you really can't afford. You could end up paying for features that sound great, but that you don't really need.

But if you do your research, shop around and stick to a budget, you can find affordable life insurance coverage.

There are a number of factors that determine the cost of life insurance. These include:

- The type of policy — term, whole, universal
- The amount of coverage you get
- How long you want coverage (if you're buying term)
- Your age
- Your gender
- Your health
- Your job
- Where you live
- The insurance company you buy from

- Whether you opt for additional features — called riders — on the policy

**Myth #3: I have to take a medical exam**. Most of today's life insurers have policies available that do not require traditional underwriting or medical exams.

These policies are often called **Guaranteed Issue** or **Simplified Issue**. A Guaranteed Issue policy is one in which everybody who applies automatically qualifies for coverage, provided they don't exceed a certain age. A Simplified Issue policy is one that requires you to fill out a medical questionnaire instead of an exam. Your responses determine if you qualify for coverage.

There are limitations to these types of insurance, such as the coverage amount you can apply for. There are also stricter age limits.

**Myth #4: The policy can only insure the person who buys it**. It's true most life insurance polices are owned by the same person they insure. But there are several scenarios in which the owner of the policy is different than the person it insures.

That doesn't mean you can buy a policy that insures your best friend or neighbor — unless there's a financial reason to do so. But you can own a policy on the life of a person whose death would have have a material effect on you. This is typically a spouse, child, or parent.

Beyond relatives, business partners often buy and own life insurance policies on each other to ensure their companies can survive the death of an owner. Some businesses even own policies on key employees identified as being critical to the success of the company.

Another common estate planning strategy is to set up a trust that purchases a life insurance policy and also serves as the beneficiary. This is used to keep the life insurance policy out of the insured's personal estate.

**Myth #5: Claim settlement is a hassle and the insurance company can deny the payout or hold a portion back**. The insurance industry as a whole has developed a reputation for not wanting to pay claims. Some of that is deserved, especially in the area of health insurance.

Life insurance is different than other types. A claim is paid if the insured person dies. This typically isn't difficult to prove. It usually only requires a death certificate. If there's uncertainty about whether a person has died, a court will have to declare them legally dead first

A rare scenario in which a claim may be denied is if the insured dies while committing a crime.

Claims can also be denied for deaths caused by suicide. However, this typically only applies in the first two years of the policy. After that, suicide is usually treated like other causes of death.

A claim could also be denied if the insurance company finds material misrepresentations on the application during the policy's contestability period. For example, if the insured's age or health condition was not accurate on the application and the insurance company discovers this during the contestability period, a claim can be denied. Once this period expires, the insurance company has no legal recourse if it finds inaccurate application information. Contestability periods are typically the first two years from the date of issue.

Also keep in mind that if the policy was canceled or surrendered before the insured's death, the insurer has no obligation to pay a claim. This is also true if premium payments were not up to date.

In any event in which an insured has died and a claim is denied, the insurance company returns the amount of premium paid during the life of the policy.

Life insurers understand that grieving survivors don't want to go through too much effort to receive their benefit. Many have introduced online claims processes that require minimal effort.

*Myths about who needs life insurance*

**Myth #6: I don't need life insurance if I am young and healthy**. Young and healthy people pass away every day. I'm not saying that as a scare tactic to change your mind; just stating a fact. According to the Centers for Disease Control, the leading cause of death for people between the ages of 15 and 44 is "unintentional injury," i.e. accidents.

Potentially fatal conditions like cancer, heart disease and pregnancy complications often strike otherwise healthy people without warning. You probably don't need to be reminded of the damage COVID-19 did to otherwise young and healthy people, but I'll do so anyway.

Being young and healthy is the best time to buy life insurance. It's never going to cost less than it will now. Wait too long, and it will be more expensive and harder to qualify. You may even become uninsurable if your health takes a bad turn.

**Myth #7: Life insurance is only for those with dependents**. You don't necessarily need a family to benefit from life insurance.

First, consider the cost of your untimely death, even if you're single with no children:

- Your parents or other family members will probably want to have a funeral, which will cost money.
- You may also have debts that your estate will have to repay, a task made easier with life insurance proceeds.
- If you have a business, whether a sole proprietorship or partnership, life insurance benefits can help with the transition after your passing.

Also, check out the "living benefits" I cover in Myth No. #16. Policy cash value can help you build tax-free wealth for the future. Accelerated benefit riders can help you preserve wealth in the event of a serious illness or injury.

You may have a family later in life. If so, all you have to do is change the beneficiary, which is easy and doesn't affect the policy coverage.

If not, you can designate other family members or even a favorite charity(s) as the policy's beneficiary.

**Myth #8: Stay-at-home parents don't need life insurance.** Stay-at-home parents may not get paid, but the child care they're providing for "free" will cost money if they die unexpectedly.

The average national cost of daycare in 2022 was $284 — per child. If your stay-at-home partner takes care of two kids, using this current average, your annual daycare expenses will be over $28,000 if he or she died. Even if you live in Arkansas, the least expensive state for daycare, caring for those two children would cost nearly $13,000 a year.

Keep in mind that's what it costs *today*. Inflation tends to be higher for child care than for other regular household expenses.

Stay-at-home parents also perform a bulk of other tasks such as cleaning and cooking, which the surviving partner may have to outsource. You will also have funeral costs to consider.

**Myth #9: Life insurance is only for the primary breadwinner.** It's true that replacing lost income is one of the primary reasons for having life insurance. But the death of any family member can affect survivors financially, in addition to emotionally.

Anybody whose death will create immediate and ongoing expenses you don't currently have, or who generates any amount of household income that you will lose, should have life insurance.

**Myth #10: I don't need life insurance if I have no debt.** This myth ignores two realities.

First, there's no guarantee you won't have debt in the future. Even if you're frugal and spend within your means, bad things sometimes happen. You might ring up some credit card debt or have an outstanding loan balance at some point. If you buy a house, you'll probably have a mortgage to pay back.

Also consider that untimely deaths are often preceded by extensive medical care. If you died as the result of an accident or serious illness, you may spend several days and even months in the hospital, not to mention doctor visits, ambulance services, emergency room expenses, travel costs and possibly hospice care. While health insurance may cover some of this, it likely won't pay for all of it, leaving those bills for whoever is in charge of settling your estate.

Second, a person's death usually affects somebody else financially. There are immediate expenses such as funeral costs, legal fees to settle an estate, grief counseling and other costs that are difficult to predict. Chance are, the income you earned while living will need to be replaced, at least for a short time. This is especially true if you operate your own business.

*Myths about who can get life insurance*

**Myth #11: I am too old to buy life insurance coverage.** It's true life insurance costs more as we age. Insurers take a deeper look at your health and other factors when underwriting applicants in their 50s, 60s and beyond.

The good news is that people are living longer. Many are staying healthier well into their advanced years.

In fact, life expectancy increases as we age. It's true. According to the Centers for Disease Control, at birth the average American is expected to live until just under age 79. But once you reach age 65, you're expected to make it until at least 85.

Life insurers have taken note of this. They're in the business of managing risk. And provided a 65-year-old is in decent health, it's not as risky to insure them today as it used to be. Statistics say they'll likely live another 20 years.

So over the years, insurers have expanded their qualifications to include seniors.

Even if you find it difficult to qualify for traditional life insurance because of your age, there are a number of group life insurance options and Guaranteed Issue policies that can provide at least some coverage.

**Myth #12: My preexisting condition will disqualify me from life insurance coverage.** This may have been true years ago. But advances in treatments and disease management means insurers are more willing to cover people with conditions like cancer, diabetes and even HIV.

Keep in mind that while a pre-existing condition does not necessarily prevent you from getting life insurance, it may increase your cost compared to similar applicants with no-preexisting conditions.

One person's pre-existing condition will not be treated the same as the same condition on another person by underwriters. They will review the seriousness and duration of your condition, as well as how it's being treated.

For example, cancer that has been in remission for several years will be looked at more favorably than if a person had just completed chemotherapy. The same is true if you're a diabetic who regularly exercises and maintains your weight and glucose levels.

The best way to get affordable life insurance with a pre-existing condition is to shop around. Insurers have varying underwriting standards. One company may balk at insuring somebody who has had open heart surgery, while another could approve coverage if the same applicant maintains an acceptable weight, cholesterol and blood pressure.

*Myths about how much life insurance I need*

**Myth #13: My life insurance coverage only needs to be twice my annual salary.** Determining how much coverage you should have is often more complicated than multiplying your current salary.

Assume you're a typical adult with a spouse and children, and you are the primary breadwinner. If your benefit equals twice your current salary, it will likely run out in less than two years.

It will take even less time to run out when the cost of your funeral, medical bills and other debts erode the policy proceeds. Plus, if there are young children, a family's expenses will only grow over time up to and including money to help finance college.

Also keep in mind that basing your death benefit on what you earn today doesn't account for the potential to earn more money in the future. Say you receive a promotion in five years. When this happens in most families, they up their lifestyle. The benefit you bought at your old salary times two won't help much if you pass away after getting that promotion and taking on more expenses.

This is why most experts suggest, at minimum, getting coverage equal to six to 10 times your current salary.

It's also strongly suggested that you do a complete needs assessment rather than just settling on a random amount.

A needs assessment will help you determine an adequate coverage amount by factoring:

- Your current income
- Your potential future income
- Current assets and debts
- Current and future household expenses
- Inflation
- Immediate expenses that will arise upon your death
- Financial goals such as saving for college, paying off the mortgage and saving for retirement

Doing this exercise will help you and your family arrive at a specific coverage amount that will better ensure adequate protection and financial security if the worst happens.

**Myth #14: My company covers me, so I don't need another policy.** People often get group life insurance through their employers or professional associations.

Group life coverage is typically cheaper than an individual policy. It's also easier to obtain because it usually does not require underwriting.

Participating in a group life insurance plan is a good way to supplement your coverage at a reasonable cost. But you should also own an individual policy to ensure that you have adequate coverage.

For starters, group plans are not meant to fulfill all of your insurance needs. They are designed to provide a worthwhile benefit, either to employees or group members. The maximum benefit amount is usually a base amount for all participants, such as $100,000. Employer policies often limit you to a maximum based on your salary (e.g. 3x your current income).

Depending on the needs of your surviving family, your life insurance may need to be 10 times to 15 times your current income.

Another reason you need more than just an employer provided policy is because group plans typically don't offer the living benefits I write about in Myth #16.

Plus, life insurance issued through a group plan is contingent on being employed by the company sponsoring the plan. If that changes, you lose your coverage.

There is also usually an annual renewal process for group plans. There is no guarantee that the employer, organization or the insurance company will renew the group coverage. At any time, your rates can increase under group insurance.

### *Myths about the usefulness of life insurance as a financial asset*

**Myth #15: Life insurance is only meant for funeral and burial costs.** This is only true for a small percentage of people who have no dependents and little to no assets. Their only financial concern about dying is ensuring that loved ones don't have to pay for a funeral and burial out of their own pockets.

If you're reading this book, your finances are far more complicated. Paying for a funeral may be the least of your surviving family's financial concerns.

As I've already written and probably will some more, life insurance is designed to replace lost income from the loss of somebody still earning money. It's designed to cover big expenses that would have arisen later on in life, such as college funding and retirement. It's a potential savings vehicle, a way to save on taxes, and a financial tool to build and preserve generational wealth.

**Myth #16: Life Insurance is only useful after my death.** I've teased this section a couple of times, so here goes.

Today's life insurance policies offer a number of "living benefits." As the name implies, these are features you might find useful while you're still among the living.

Some are automatically included in a policy. Some are available for an extra cost. They may vary by the state you live in and the insurance company you use.

Some of these living benefits include:

**Cash value that you can withdraw or borrow against.** Many permanent life insurance policies, such as whole life, build cash value over time. Life insurance cash value is available to you as if it were your own savings account. You can withdraw cash value or borrow and repay it later. This money can be used for a variety of purposes. Plus, it's usually tax-free money.

Many companies also have riders or built-in features that enable you to **access part of the policy's death benefit** if you:

- Require long-term care
- Suffer a qualifying disability
- Are diagnosed with a qualifying chronic, critical, or terminal illness

**Myth #17: I don't need life insurance if I have savings.** Over many years, you managed to save your money. $100 here, $50 there. You watched it add up and earn interest. Maybe you invested some of it and saw it grow even more.

All the while, you ignored all the temptations to spend that money elsewhere, on some immediate gratification. Saving money is an admirable pursuit.

So if I may be bold: Why would you be ok to let all that money disappear in way less time than it took to save it? When a person dies and leaves dependents with financial obligations, money erodes very quickly. Your surviving loved ones may discover that you didn't have as much saved as you thought you did. Plus, I'm guessing you saved that money for something other than to replace your income if you die.

All it takes to preserve much of, if not all of, that savings and to let it grow more if you pass away is to use the same philosophy you used to save it in the first place.

You pay a premium amount to an insurance company, be it monthly, quarterly or annually. With the first payment, you have an instant death benefit should something happen to you. This benefit is much larger than the amount of premium you're paying.

Plus, if you buy whole life or other permanent policy, your life insurance becomes another vehicle to save even more money that you can use in the future.

So maybe you don't need life insurance if you have savings, but you'll be better off in the long run if you have both.

**Myth #18: I can get better returns from other investment vehicles**. This might be true on the surface. But when comparing life insurance to other financial tools, you also have to consider its other benefits.

- Life insurance offers a death benefit plus the accelerated benefits for serious illness or injury.
- Unlike most investment vehicles, life insurance proceeds are almost always tax-free.

- Most life insurance policies that build cash value have safeguards in place so they never lose value due to market losses.

### Myths about permanent life insurance

**Myth #19: You only need term life insurance.** This depends on how a person defines need. If you're only concerned with income replacement while your children are living at home or for a specific number of years, this might — might — be true.

If, on the other hand, you have an estate you want to pass along efficiently to the next generation, that need will probably never go away. The same is true if you have a child with a disability who will need long-term care after you have passed away.

So why only buy a term policy that expires when you can get permanent insurance that stays active as long as you pay the required premium?

**Myth #20: Permanent life insurance is only for the wealthy.** People used to think the same thing about the stock market until 401(k) plans came along to help millions of workers save and invest for retirement. Now everybody who participates in these plans is an investor.

Permanent life insurance is such a versatile financial tool it can benefit non-affluent people as well as the wealthy, both during their lives and after they're gone.

## MOVING ON TO THE TRUTH OF LIFE INSURANCE

Hopefully I've dispelled the falsehoods surrounding life insurance.

Most of this book will advise you on dealing with the certainty of taxes. That is, after all, the secondary title: "Unlocking Tax-Free Financial Abundance." It's also the title of this chapter: "Tax-Efficient Wealth Building: The Potential of Life Insurance."

Before I continue with that lesson, I want to write briefly about death, the other certainty in life Franklin mentioned in his letter to Le Roy.

Yes, death is certain. But uncertainty comes because we typically don't know when our death will occur. Our own passing could happen in five minutes, five years, five decades. Despite the 100 percent certainty of dying, the actual time it arrives often comes as a shock to the people around us. The loss of life of a loved one or business partner upends our own lives.

This is and always will be the primary purpose of life insurance. You need to be insured to financially assist the important people in your life in the event that you die tomorrow and can no longer provide for them. You also need insurance on those people to help you cope financially.

If for no other reason, have life insurance to protect each other financially from the unpredictable certainty of death.

## THE SMARTPHONE OF THE FINANCIAL WORLD

The point of this book, however, is to help you understand there's greater value in owning life insurance than just providing a death benefit.

In the old days, I might have compared the value and versatility of life insurance to a Swiss army knife. The main purpose of the gadget is as a knife, but it also comes with an array of tools, including a bottle opener, nail file and corkscrew.

The better analogy for modern times is that today's life insurance is like a smartphone.

The primary purpose of a phone is to verbally communicate with people. Today, most people don't even use their phones to talk. They use them instead to text and email, as well as for ordering food, tracking their children, checking the weather, adjusting their thermostat, and watching TV, among hundreds of other potential uses.

Here, I've compiled a list of some of the ways life insurance can help you build wealth on a tax-efficient basis.

**Life insurance can protect your family's quality of life**

One of the tragedies of losing a parent is the negative impact it can have on the surviving parent and children.

There are countless stories of hardworking, successful families who were forced to alter their lifestyle after the death of a parent. With only one income, and with debt to repay and not enough life insurance to help out, widowed families often have to move out of their homes. Often they're forced to rent smaller living quarters or move to an area with a lower cost of living. Sometimes that even includes the surviving spouse — and their children — moving back in with their parents.

Being uprooted in this way has a detrimental effect on a child's ability to learn, succeed and prepare for life. It can also negatively impact the life and career of the surviving parent.

### Life insurance can help finance college

If you or your spouse/partner die before your children reach college, you can better ensure they can afford it with life insurance. Some of the death benefit can be set aside to pay some or all of the tuition.

I've also mentioned cash value life insurance several times in this chapter. One of the most popular uses of a policy's cash value is to help parents pay for their children's college education.

Using your life insurance policy can help minimize the amount of student loan debt your kids borrow. Saving money in a life insurance policy also offers more flexibility than using a 529 college funding plan.

This is an important part of building generational wealth. Many of the highest paying jobs in our economy require college degrees. If kids can't afford college or if they're weighed down by large student loan debt, it hinders their ability to build their own wealth as adults.

## Life insurance can provide future savings

Once the debts, immediate expenses and ongoing items are covered, beneficiaries of a life insurance policy can set aside the rest in a savings account.

In addition to college, money in savings can be used in a number of ways to build and protect generational wealth. Beneficiaries could use that savings:

- As an emergency fund to minimize the use of debt in the future.
- To invest in a variety of financial vehicles, such as annuities, mutual funds or more life insurance.
- To start a business that can be passed down to future generations.
- To purchase real estate.

## Life insurance can pay your estate taxes

The estate tax doesn't currently apply to many families. But if you're passing down a rather large estate to the next generation, the IRS might demand a percentage of it.

The estate tax is a tax on the transfer property at your death. Whether you owe the tax and how much you owe depends on the fair market value of your entire estate at the time of your death.

Estates valued at $12.92 million or less in 2023 were exempt from federal estate taxes. The tax rates begin at 18 percent up to the current top tax rate of 40 percent on any value of your estate above $13.92 million.

So, for example, if you had an estate valued at $15 million, the IRS will claim $777,800 in taxes.

Several states also have their own estate tax rules.

There are two issues with estate taxes. First, your heirs will lose a significant chunk of what you worked hard to provide for them.

Second, if your estate doesn't have enough liquidity to cover the estate tax bill, your heirs may have to sell assets in order to cover it. This might mean selling real estate, farmland or even a business just to square themselves with the tax collectors.

You can solve both problems with adequate life insurance. Establish a death benefit that at least covers the estate tax bill and your heirs can inherit the full estate without divesting any of it to pay taxes.

**Life insurance can pay off estate debt**

So you want to leave your home, or your business, or another asset, to your heirs. But each of those entities has a loan balance. That debt goes with the asset when it's passed to the next generation.

Just as with estate taxes, beneficiaries often have little choice but selling an inherited asset in order to pay the debt on that inheritance. This erodes the wealth you intended to pass on.

The solution — if you've been paying attention — is life insurance. Your heirs can use the life insurance benefit to pay off outstanding loan balances. They therefore inherit the full value of your estate.

## Life insurance proceeds can be placed in a trust

If you're like a lot of parents who don't exactly trust your kids to manage wealth wisely, you can name a trust fund as the policy's beneficiary. This enables you to leave instructions on how the money should be disbursed and used. You can designate the funds for college. You can even have it invested by a professional and even set up a conservative withdrawal strategy to create multi-generational wealth.

## Permanent life insurance can help you cut your tax bill

There are a number of planning strategies using life insurance that can help you reduce your taxes while you're alive and minimize the tax obligations of your beneficiaries after you have passed. This includes tapping into a policy's cash value on a tax-free basis, and creating a tax-free inheritance for your loved ones. I will explain these strategies in more details in the subsequent chapters of this book.

## Chapter 1 summary

Death and taxes may be the only certainties in life, but you lessen the burden they cause using life insurance.

Life insurance is one of the most versatile financial tools available. It provides flexibility that enables you to determine how much to buy, how long you want to be covered, and to who you designate the benefits. With that versatility and flexibility, life insurance can help you build and preserve wealth while minimizing financial risks, all in a tax-efficient manner.

You'll read a number of wealth planning strategies in the remaining chapters. In the next chapter, I'll cover the crucial role life insurance plays as an investment tool, especially in the context of the current financial climate.

# ANALYZING THE ROLE OF LIFE INSURANCE IN YOUR FINANCIAL PORTFOLIO

*"If a child, a spouse, a life partner or a parent depends on you and your income, you need life insurance."*

— Suze Orman

D eath and taxes may be certainties. The economy? That's another story.

Like death, we know that economic downturns and recessions are just part of life. But despite the best efforts of experts to predict movements in the domestic and global economy, we rarely know just when those downturns might occur. Furthermore, we are often not prepared for the severity of an impending downturn.

## WHAT GOES UP, ALWAYS COMES DOWN

This is especially true if we've been riding the wave of good fortune for many years.

If you know your U.S. history, you know that the 1920s were a booming period for the nation. That is, until the stock market crashed and we plunged into a decade-long depression that affected every American in some way. At its worst point, nearly a quarter of the U.S. workforce was unemployed. And domestic GDP plummeted more than 26 percent from its highest to its lowest point.

The post-World War II years were prosperous for the nation, with only a few short, minor recessions interrupting the flow of money during the 1950s and 1960s. Then, between 1969 and 1981, the country experienced four recessions. Inflation and unemployment both hit double digits. There were two major energy crises during this time, as well as a stock market crash.

But beginning in the early to mid 1980s, the U.S. was living large. The 1990s, especially, was a time of unprecedented economic growth. That came to a grinding halt with the dot-com bust and the first years of the war on terrorism. The S&P 500 suffered three consecutive years of double-digit annual losses. By the end of 2002, the stock market lost nearly half of its value from where it started the 21st century. Yikes!

But we weren't done with bad times. Just as the country had recovered from that horrendous period came the subprime mortgage crisis of 2007-2008. The housing bubble collapsed, leading to a wave of foreclosures and plummeting home values.

Oil and food prices soared. Large financial institutions and automakers needed government bailouts to avoid permanent closure. And all of that led to the S&P 500 shedding 38.5 percent of its value in one calendar year, 2008.

The 2010s were mostly strong economically. Then in March 2020 the world changed forever as a strange virus shut down normal economic activity across the entire globe.

As I write this, the global economy is still recovering from the COVID-19 pandemic. Though there has been positive news for the previous few years, another recession is on the horizon as there remain many disconcerting economic trends, including:

- The war between Russia and Ukraine and its effect on the global food market and the possibility of a conflict involving more nations. And as I finish this book, a war has begun in Israel with its larger impact still unknown.
- Inflation that remains stubbornly high in many countries following the pandemic.
- The lack of affordable housing and the inability of builders to keep up with housing demand has resulted in more families spending a greater share of their incomes on rent or mortgage payments. Making the problem worse for homebuyers is that 30-year mortgage rates soared from between 2-3 percent to over 7 percent in the previous two years.
- The possibility that global markets may experience prolonged stagnation with so much turmoil occurring in the world.

- Continued supply chain disruptions that originated during the pandemic.
- Weak job recovery and rising poverty.
- Weak retail sales in the U.S.
- Record amount of debt carried by both the U.S. government and the nation's households.
- A series of natural disasters, including floods, droughts, extreme heat, damaging storms and wildfires. Every new disaster brings calls for greater climate action. Regardless of how the world responds, the economic impact will be tangible.

Those are the ones I could think of from following the news. There are probably many more lurking in the shadows.

## YES, WE'RE STILL TALKING ABOUT LIFE INSURANCE

So what does all this economic news have to do with buying life insurance, you may be asking?

My answer is this: So much of what happens in our lives is outside of our control. The economy is chief among the stuff that often makes life challenging to navigate.

The best way to handle the unknowns is to take care of the stuff you can control. Be as prepared as possible to weather these downturns.

The purchase of life insurance may be a personal decision. But the risks associated with the domestic and international economies are a critical reason why people who depend on you must be protected financially.

## WHY WE DON'T GET THIS DONE SOONER

In my experience, most people are responsible enough to understand this. They know deep down they need life insurance. In some cases, they realize they need more than they own.

Part of our neglect in buying life insurance is that nobody is forcing us, like with other types of insurance. Your mortgage company insists you have homeowners insurance to protect their loan. State governments mandate auto insurance if you're going to drive.

Even though health insurance is no longer required by the federal government, most people have it, especially those with families. It's much easier, after all, to see the need to prepare for sickness and injury than it is for death.

I suspect that even if other types of insurance were not mandated, most people would get them. It's easier to imagine a house fire, auto accident or broken leg that nobody wants to pay full price to repair, than it is to consider an early death.

Discussing one's own mortality is difficult for many people. It can also be unsettling for a spouse or loved one to imagine life without you. This is one of the key reasons why otherwise responsible people procrastinate on such an important task.

It's also easy to just forget about doing it — until it's too late. Life is busy. Our jobs, families, household chores, kids' activities, and recreational life take up the bulk of our waking hours. Fitting in a life insurance discussion proves challenging for many.

It certainly doesn't help that there's often a considerable time commitment when applying for life insurance. There are a number of decisions to consider. What type of life insurance should you buy? How much should you get? How long do you really need to be covered? Are there other benefits we should add to our policy?

Answering these questions requires significant research or a lengthy discussion with a licensed insurance professional. Assessing your coverage needs requires a complete review of your current finances and future goals.

Completing the application and undergoing a medical exam also take time, though as a I mentioned in the previous chapter, many insurers have streamlined these processes.

In the previous chapter I also wrote about the myth of how much life insurance costs. This is another reason people avoid the issue. In fact, one recent study revealed that 80 percent of consumers overestimate the cost of a life insurance policy.

## THE CONSEQUENCES OF INADEQUATE COVERAGE

Regardless of the reasons, being uninsured or underinsured causes an array of consequences.

Life insurance was designed to replace lost income. People typically get it to financially provide for loved ones if they pass away unexpectedly.

In most cases, beneficiaries receive a one-time death benefit. It happens too often that the death benefit isn't big enough to last more than a year or so.

If your survivors can't maintain their current lifestyle, they also can't build for the future.

It's important to think about what it will cost to provide for your survivors if you're not there to help support them. When determining how much life insurance you need, don't under-statement these needs and don't just pull a number out of the air. Consider the cost of:

- Covering your house payment or rent
- Settling debts that need repayment even if you die
- Child care
- Premiums on medical insurance that your employer is currently subsidizing
- College tuition for your children
- Retirement savings for your surviving spouse

One last point to make: The legacy of the deceased is also at stake. If you die without leaving enough for survivors to continue living well, they may grow frustrated, even resentful toward you. The happy memories they may have had of you will be replaced with feelings of neglect as they move to a less expensive house, cut back on extras like vacations, and struggle with an uncertain future.

## ADDITIONAL REASONS TO INVEST IN LIFE INSURANCE

Avoiding the financial consequences of having no coverage is certainly a motivating factor to buying life insurance. But it shouldn't be the only one. As I've written and will be repeating throughout this book, life insurance is one of the versatile and valuable financial tools available to people of all incomes.

**Supplementing your retirement income with policy cash value.** The tax code gives people a way to save for retirement while reducing their current tax bills. This is through 401(k) plans, IRAs and a host of other tax-advantaged retirement plans.

Few people argue the merits of these plans. The money you contribute in a calendar year is deducted from your taxable income. In addition, your employer can contribute to your retirement as well.

There are a few limitations, however. The IRS limits how much you can contribute each year. It also mandates when you're allowed to access retirement plan money without penalty.

Life insurance has none of these limitations or mandates. You can contribute as much as the policy will allow without IRS limits. There are also no age restrictions. You can withdraw funds anytime as long as there is sufficient cash value in the policy.

Also, because life insurance withdrawals are not taxable, they don't impact the formula the IRS uses to determine whether to tax your Social Security benefits.

I will analyze how life insurance compares with traditional retirement plans in Chapter 7.

**Getting in the habit of saving**. This is especially true if you buy a permanent policy with a cash value component. Each premium payment you make is similar to putting money in a savings account. The more money you put toward your policy, the more you save and the more cash value you can accumulate for future needs.

**Gaining peace of mind**. It's a great feeling to know you've done what you can to prepare for the worst. You feel better about yourself and your future. Having a sufficient amount of life insurance takes a lot of the "what-ifs" out of the complexity and uncertainty of life.

## ADVANTAGES OF PERMANENT LIFE INSURANCE

One of the first decisions you'll have to make is whether to buy term insurance or one of the types of permanent life insurance.

Most people will default to term. This is because, as I've covered, term life insurance is considerably less expensive than permanent coverage. At the same time, permanent life insurance offers advantages that term insurance does not.

The main benefit of permanent life insurance is the ability to maintain coverage for your entire life. As long as you keep your permanent policy active, you don't have to reapply or go through underwriting. Plus, you'll be paying roughly the same amount of premium for the life of the policy instead of reapplying later in life at a higher amount.

Other potential benefits of permanent life insurance include:

**Potential cash value**. Permanent life insurance policies build cash value. The cash value is the amount of premium you paid that is not needed to cover the insurance company's cost to insure you. That cash value earns interest.

**Potential dividends on whole life insurance**. There is a type of whole life insurance called a participating policy, which pays a dividend to the policy owner. This dividend is paid by the insurance company to owners based on their annual earnings. Dividends are often used to pay ahead on premium or to increase the cash value of the policy. Some policy owners like to receive cash instead.

**The tax treatment**. The cash value inside the policy grows tax-deferred, plus you can withdraw or borrow some of the cash value on a tax-free basis. The policy's death benefit is not taxable to whoever receives it.

**Accelerated benefits**. Many permanent policies offer what are called living benefits that you can take advantage of before you die. They come in the form of optional policy riders or automatically included features. They're potentially useful if you:

- Require long-term care
- Suffer a qualifying disability
- Are diagnosed with a qualifying chronic, critical, or terminal illness

## DISADVANTAGES OF PERMANENT LIFE INSURANCE

The main disadvantage of permanent life insurance is that it is considerably more expensive than a similar term policy.

This is the price you pay for having a lifetime death benefit, which is guaranteed provided you pay the necessary premiums. What it costs the insurance company to provide lifetime guarantees is much higher than temporary term benefits.

Another potential disadvantage of permanent life insurance is people sometimes discover they don't need life insurance coverage for their entire life, or at least not as much as they age. If you discover this later in life, it won't help much if you spent years paying higher premiums than you would have had you elected term insurance.


## THE PROS AND CONS OF TERM LIFE INSURANCE

Term life insurance has a number of advantages and disadvantages as well.

The chief advantage is the cost. A life insurance policy that only covers a specific term instead of a person's entire less means less risk for the insurance company. Less risk means the company can charge less. You can save even more by buying term when you're young and healthy.

Term life also provides flexibility. Most insurers offer term periods of 10, 20 and 30 years. Therefore you can choose a term based on your need and budget.

Another advantage is that insurers typically offer conversion programs, giving you the ability to convert a term policy to permanent insurance. This provides the ability to pay a lower premium when you're starting out in life and perhaps can't afford permanent insurance, then taking on the higher premiums of a permanent policy later when your income grows.

The main disadvantage of term life insurance is that it doesn't accumulate cash value. All of your premium goes toward covering the cost of insuring your life.

Plus, if you're still alive when the term ends, the policy simply lapses and you and your beneficiaries don't see any money. The majority of term policies never pay out a death benefit. They either expire, lapse, get replaced or are converted to permanent insurance.

## LIFE INSURANCE MISTAKES TO AVOID

Beside being inadequately covered, there are several other mistakes you can make when considering life insurance. Here are a few of the key ones to avoid:

**Waiting too long to get insurance.** Life insurance will cost more with every year you age. Health issues that can creep up as you age will also add to your premium amount.

You might not need life insurance right now. But you should at least consider getting a policy now because you might need it later, when it will cost more. Keep in mind that:

- You can start out with an affordable term policy and convert it to a permanent policy later when you have more money and greater needs.
- You can cancel a term policy at any time and replace it with a different type of coverage if necessary.
- You can keep an existing policy and simply buy another separate policy to supplement your coverage when greater need arises.
- Many life insurance polices have a feature where you can add coverage after you've owned your policy for several years. These purchase options typically do not require additional underwriting, though you will pay a higher premium for the increased coverage.

**Relying on group life insurance.** Insurance experts advise against making a group life insurance policy your only coverage, though it's an affordable way to reinforce your overall coverage. Group policies are usually contingent on employment or membership in an organization. If that changes, you likely lose your group coverage. Doing so puts you at risk of losing your coverage because of a change in jobs. It's also unlikely for a group plan to provide enough coverage to for your individual situation.

**Not covering a non-working spouse.** You may think a spouse who doesn't work or who makes much less than you doesn't need life insurance. You may not be concerned with replacing your spouse's income if they die, but an untimely death would potentially create other financial needs. You would want to cover funeral costs without relying on your savings. Plus, the amount of time you need to grieve your spouse's loss may exceed the paid time off your employer would offer. Most importantly, you should consider the cost of replacing tasks your spouse performs, such as child care.

**Not comparison shopping.** Many companies sell life insurance, some with names you've heard of and perhaps a few obscure ones. It's a competitive market, which means choices for you in terms of features and premium costs. You're advised to never settle for the first choice you see or recommendation you receive.

**Automatically buying the cheapest policy.** There is more to comparison shopping than just cost. Before you sign the contract, make sure you're getting the best value.

First, since the cheapest options is likely going to be a term policy with the shortest term, make sure that meets your immediate and long-term needs. Ask yourself:

- Do my needs merit consideration of a permanent policy instead?
- Does the cheap policy allow me to convert it to permanent later?
- Did I miss out on key riders and other living benefits by defaulting to the cheapest option?
- Should I opt for a longer term policy?
- What does the option I'm looking at provide when the term policy expires?

You need to assess other factors that impact your coverage. These include the riders and features the policy offers. Each company's underwriting standards also differ, meaning you may get a better deal from one firm over another because they don't consider you as much of a risk.

It's important to factor in the strength, reputation, and history of the insurance company that issues the policy.

Comparison shopping for life insurance is an area where working with a licensed insurance professional can help.

**Not properly designating beneficiaries.** The policy's beneficiary(s) are the people and/or entities who are legally entitled to the death benefit. Designating beneficiaries is a critical step for every policy owner, and one of the most overlooked.

First, it's important to name more than one possible beneficiary. If you only designate one person as a beneficiary and that person dies before you, then your policy's death benefit becomes a legal issue because there will be nobody legally entitled to that money. Every policy should have one or more contingent beneficiaries, who receive the death benefit ONLY if the primary beneficiary(s) is deceased or nonexistent by the time you pass away.

Once you own your policy, regularly review those designations. You can make beneficiary changes any time by contacting the insurance company. One possible reason to change is if you get divorced, especially if you get remarried. You may not want your death benefit going to your ex-spouse while your current spouse receives nothing. You may also want to name your children as primary or contingent beneficiaries.

**Allowing premiums to lapse.** Whether you're buying term or permanent coverage, you're required to pay the necessary premiums to keep the policy active. Failing to do so will lead the insurance company to cancel your coverage. It's similar to how a lender will repossess a car or foreclose on a house if you don't make your payments on time.

If you buy term, you can typically set up an automatic withdrawal from a bank account. If you buy permanent coverage, check your policy statements each month to ensure that the amount of premium you're paying is keeping up with policy expenses.

Some types of permanent insurance, like universal life insurance, require a minimum of cash value to keep the policy active. If the cash value isn't growing at a high enough interest rate, you may need to increase the amount of premium you pay.

Check with your insurer if you might be late or fall behind payments. Many companies allow 30 to 60 day grace periods without changing the policy's guarantee.

**Borrowing too much from your policy.** Permanent life insurance policies that accumulate cash value can serve as a source of funds. You can make tax-free withdrawals or take out a policy loan up to a certain percentage of the policy's cash value and use the money for any purpose.

A risk arises if you borrow too much. Many of us have made the mistake of overdrawing our bank account, then paying a penalty fee to the bank and/or to the entity that didn't get their money from an overdrawn payment.

When it happens to a life insurance policy, borrowing too much cash value can cause the policy to lapse. If this happens, there may also be tax implications to this mistake in addition to losing your coverage.

Any amount of money withdrawn or borrowed from the cash value reduces the policy's death benefit. So, borrowing too much means a lot less money going to your beneficiaries.

## MISSING PAYMENTS AND LAPSING YOUR POLICY

Missing a payment or being late won't automatically cancel your coverage. There is usually a 30-day grace period for you to get caught up on your premium. You still have coverage during the grace period and the policy would still pay out a benefit if you died during this period.

**How long can I go without paying my premium?** This depends on whether you have term insurance or permanent insurance.

Completely missing payments on a term life insurance policy will cause it to lapse. This means you no longer have life insurance coverage.

You can typically go longer on a permanent policy. That's because the cash value accumulated in the policy supports the life insurance coverage. As long as there is sufficient cash value, your coverage will remain active.

What happens when life insurance lapses? If your policy lapses, you no longer have coverage. The insurance company is no longer contractually obligated to pay a death benefit if you die.

The good news is that you may be able to reinstate a lapsed policy, depending on how long it has been lapsed. Some companies will give you 15 to 30 days after a lapse takes place to get caught up on your premium payments and reinstate your coverage.

In addition to paying any premiums still owed, some insurers may charge interest on any past due premiums before they reinstate coverage. You may also have to attest to your current health and whether it's changed significantly since your policy went into effect.

If you have lapsed a policy and still need coverage, it's in your best interest to do everything you can to reinstate it rather than applying for new coverage. Starting all over means going through underwriting and likely paying a higher premium.

**How to minimize the risk of lapsing a policy**

You want to avoid lapsing your coverage as much as possible. Here are a few things you can to prevent that from happening:

- Make your payments an automatic, electronic deduction from your bank account.
- Eliminate riders if you're having trouble with payments. The policy typically allows you to drop any optional riders you put on the policy when you applied. Keep in mind that insurance companies typically won't

allow you to put those riders on later if you remove them.

- Take advantage of flexible premiums. If you purchased a universal life policy, you can adjust your premium amount by lowering your death benefit. You can also overpay your premium if you have extra money, which will help build cash value to support the coverage.
- Pay your premiums from within your policy, when needed. The cash value in permanent life insurance can be used to pay for premiums, on a temporary basis. You can also direct your whole life dividends toward paying premiums.
- Pay monthly instead of annually if you're having trouble covering the large yearly bill.
- Review your policy statements and keep track of your cash value. With permanent insurance, insurers typically send you monthly, quarterly or annual statements. Most insurers also provide an online dashboard you can check anytime for this information. These will show, among other information, how much cash value the policy has and the interest it is earning. By reviewing this information, you can insure your cash value is adequate to support your coverage and adjust your premium payments if necessary.

## Chapter 2 summary

Life insurance should be a critical part of nearly every household's financial plan. This is especially true in a global economy that is filled with complexity and uncertainty. Individuals and families should prepare as much as they can for these unknowns.

Then, once you have life insurance, it's important to avoid the landmine of potential mistakes that can minimize its effectiveness. Chief among these mistakes is allowing your coverage to lapse due to missing payments or underfunding your policy.

While this chapter provided a general overview of the importance of life insurance, the remaining chapters will offer specific strategies and scenarios for how to use life insurance to build and preserve wealth.

That begins with Chapter 3, which covers various aspects of using life insurance as a means to achieve tax-free growth.

# X-FACTOR BENEFITS: HOW LIFE INSURANCE STANDS APART

---

*"Life insurance can give you financial security when everyone else is in panic mode."*

— DAVID ANGWAY

---

I'm afraid I have to return to one of Ben Franklin's certainties in this chapter: Taxes.

I get it. Other than IRS agents and tax preparers, nobody enjoys the topic of taxes. But it's important that you understand how taxes affect your wealth and how to minimize that impact. I promise this chapter won't dwell on the nuts and bolts of tax policy. Instead, I intend to cover legal ways you can minimize and/or defer tax obligations as you build wealth for the future.

You're no doubt aware that the U.S. tax code is one of the most complex rule books that exists. For many people, it's easier to understand quantum physics than tax law. It's not surprising why that is. After all, the U.S. economy is also complex, arguably the most intricate in the world. Capitalists have for generations invented new ways to earn, save, invest and accumulate money, and they seem to create more every day. The IRS always wants their cut of that money, not to mention the politicians whose job it is to spend it.

## TAXES ARE NOT CREATED EQUAL

The good news is you don't have to know everything in the tax code. For the sake of building wealth, a good place to start is to understand the different ways taxes are assessed on different assets and investment types.

In general, there are three types of tax treatments on assets and investments:

- Fully taxable
- Tax-deferred
- Tax-free

A fully taxable investment vehicle is one that receives no special tax treatment in the tax code. You don't receive tax benefits for making the investment. Any income generated while you own the asset is fully taxed. In addition, you will either pay taxes on the growth in value of the investment each year, or you will pay a capital gains tax on the asset when you sell it.

A capital gain is basically the difference between what you invested and what the asset is worth when the tax bill is assessed. For example, if you purchased $10,000 worth of stock in a company, then sold it for $50,000 years later, you would be assessed a capital gain of $40,000 ($50,000 - $10,000). You would be required to pay a capital gains tax on that $40,000.

On the opposite end of the spectrum is a tax-free investment. These are investments that the government encourages people to invest in by removing tax obligations.

One well-known example is a Roth retirement account. To encourage people to save money for retirement, these accounts grow on a tax-free basis and, most important, you will pay no income taxes on the money you withdraw as income. Certain municipal bonds generate tax-free interest as well, as a way to induce people to invest in schools and other government capital projects.

## WHAT IS A TAX-DEFERRED INVESTMENT?

In between tax-free and fully taxable is tax-deferral.

Tax-deferral is when you have an asset that allows you to earn money today but pay taxes at a later date. When you invest in a tax-deferred asset or account, you don't pay taxes on the interest growth that accrues. Instead, you defer your tax liability until later, such as when you withdraw money from the account.

Accounts designed to help people save for retirement are the most common tax-deferred accounts. These include 401(k) plans, Individual Retirement Accounts (IRAs) and annuities. In each example, money inside those accounts grow tax-deferred. You won't pay taxes on these accounts until you begin withdrawing retirement income.

Why is tax deferral a benefit? The main reason is that deferring taxes maximizes the growth potential from compounding interest.

Compounding interest is when the interest you earn today gets added to your account value and reinvested, which then maximizes the balance from which you can earn additional interest. Here's a quick example of how compounding interest works.

Say you invest $10,000 a year that earns 10 percent interest. After the first year, this hypothetical account would have $11,000 ($10,000 + 10%).

Without compounding interest, the $1,000 in interest you earned would essentially be set aside. The next year, you would invest $10,000 and you would earn 10 percent interest on $20,000, which would equal $2,000.

With compounding interest, your second-year investment would be added to your $11,000 account value. That gives you $21,000. Ten percent interest on $21,000 is $2,100, or an extra $100. Over time, the power of compounding greatly increases your accumulation potential. In short, you earn interest on your interest, in addition to your original principal.

Without tax-deferral, the potential of compound interest is minimized. That's because the tax payment coming out of your account won't earn interest. With tax-deferral, you'll earn interest on your original investment plus whatever interest it's already earned.

Keep in mind that in exchange for tax deferral, there are also limitations. The IRS, after all, doesn't want people deferring taxes on unlimited resources.

In the case of tax-deferred retirement plans, the IRS limits how much you can contribute to your plans each year. In addition, you can't withdraw the money until you reach 59 1/2 without paying a steep tax penalty, though you can take out a loan. However, loaned funds must be repaid within a certain time period or those funds will also be subjected to a tax penalty.

In addition, the IRS won't allow you to hold the money in a tax-deferred account forever. Beginning when you reach age 70 1/2, you have to take a Required Minimum Distribution (RMD) each year. An RMD is equal to a percentage of the account's overall value based on your age.

## MAXIMIZE YOUR SAVINGS WITH TAX-EFFICIENT STRATEGIES

Taxes often diminish your investment returns. That's why it's important to consider the tax implications of any investment strategy. You can't just analyze the interest earned on an investment to assess its effectiveness in meeting your financial goals. After all, an asset that generates an 8 percent return but with a high tax bill may actually underperform a 5 percent return with no tax bill.

The higher your tax rate, the more you need a tax-efficient investment approach to meet your goals.

One of the best and simplest ways to maximize your savings while minimizing your tax burden is to contribute to tax-advantaged accounts, such as the previously mentioned 401(k) and IRA retirement savings accounts.

These and similar accounts offer a couple of tax incentives. First, you can deduct your annual contributions, up to a maximum, from your taxable income. Second, there is no tax charged on the interest or dividends during the growth phase of this account.

## HOW MUCH DO TAXES AFFECT YOUR SAVINGS?

Here are a couple of scenarios demonstrating the advantages of tax-deferred accounts.

Imagine you invest $10,000 and earn a 7 percent annual return. For this hypothetical scenario, it's assumed your tax rate is 22 percent and remains so for the life of your account.

Here's a comparison of what the value of your savings would be in a tax-deferred account, such as a 401(k) or IRA, and what it would be in a standard taxable account:

- **After 10 years, the tax-deferred account has 8 percent more** value than the comparable taxable accounts.
- **In 20 years, the tax-deferred account has provided 13 percent more** value than the taxable account would have during the same period.

- **In 30 years, you have 15 percent more money** had you invested in the tax-deferred account than you would have in the taxable account.

The results get even better if your tax rate begins at 22 percent, but drops to 15 percent at the end of each of the three investment periods. Basically, this scenario would mean you would pay a lower percentage of the income you withdraw from the income than what it was when you contributed it. In this hypothetical scenario:

- You have **19 percent more money after 10 years.**
- You have **27 percent more money after 20 years**.
- You have **35 percent more money after 30 years**.

How do the results differ so much? After all, in both scenarios you're paying taxes at some point.

For starters, the tax-deferred accounts allows you to deduct the $10,000 contribution from your taxable income in the year you make it. You can't do that in the taxable account, which means you're essentially contributing $7,800 -- instead of the full $10,000 — in the taxable account because you didn't receive a tax deduction, which equals $2,200 in the tax-deferred account.

In short, you invested with more money using a tax-deferred account, so that one got a large head start.

Second, the 7 percent return you earned each year also created a 15 percent capital gains tax on that growth. You either paid it each year or the end of each of the 10-year periods in the scenarios.

In the tax-deferred account, you pay an income tax on whatever money you withdraw each year from the account. This money is taxed essentially the same as what you earn from salary income.

## LIFE CHANGES; SO DO TAX RATES

As you consider how much of your strategy should involve this type of account, you will want to think about how your tax obligations today will compare to when you begin withdrawing income.

If you are in a higher tax bracket today than you will be when you actually have to pay taxes on your income, you'll ultimately profit from this strategy.

On the other hand, some people might find themselves in higher tax brackets in retirement than they are during the years they're making contributions to those account. This can occur in one or more of several ways:

- You end up with more taxable income during your retirement years than you did while working.
- You move to a state that has a higher income tax than the state in which you made most of your retirement plan contributions.
- The federal government raises tax rates that put you in a higher bracket.

If this happens, your investment strategy may underperform its potential. That's because a higher percentage of your income will go toward taxes in retirement than what you saved in the years you received the tax advantages of those accounts.

Of course, it's challenging if not impossible to determine with certainty what the future holds. This is especially true of the tax climate.

## DIVERSIFYING YOUR ACCOUNT TYPES

Rather than guess at what your tax rate might be in 10 to 30 years, you should consider diversifying your account types. In this context, it means having money in several accounts that have different tax treatments.

Even taxable accounts have a place in your portfolio. These are often the most accessible; you can typically withdraw money whenever you want. There is also no limit on how much you can save in a taxable account.

Tax-advantaged accounts, on the other hand, typically have limits on what you can contribute and when you can withdraw money.

Putting some of your money in a variety of taxable and tax-advantaged accounts provides flexibility, especially as you work toward other financial goals in addition to retirement.

## OTHER TYPES OF TAX-EFFICIENT INVESTMENTS

There are a number of tax-efficient investment options besides contributing money to a 401(k) or IRA. These include:

- Roth IRAs and Roth 401(k)s offer a different tax advantage than traditional versions of these accounts. With Roth versions, you don't get to deduct your contribution amount from your taxable income. However, the investments grow on a tax-free basis and, most importantly, you will pay no income taxes on the money you withdraw as income.
- Certain municipal bonds generate tax-free interest at the federal level and potentially at the state and local levels.
- Treasury bonds and Series I bonds (also called Savings Bonds) are also typically exempt from state and federal taxes.
- Tax-efficient mutual funds or exchange traded funds (ETFs) can help minimize your overall tax liability.

## ASSET LOCATION IS ALSO IMPORTANT

Where you hold securities is an important component of tax-efficient investing.

For example, you'll likely have investments that are meant to generate regular income, such as in retirement. These include high-yielding taxable bonds, bond funds and real estate investment trusts. These types of investments should generally be held in a tax-deferred account.

Investments that you are allocating for long-term growth potential might be best inside of a Roth account. That's because any growth in the account value will be free of income AND capital gains taxes. Imagine having an account that, say, triples in value over a 30-year period. When you withdraw that money, you'll owe no taxes on it if it was held in a Roth account.

Then there are the investments mentioned above that are tax-efficient on their own, such as municipal bonds. It doesn't make sense to put a tax-efficient investment in a tax-advantaged account, because you're already reaping the tax advantages. Therefore, it's best to put tax-efficient investments in a taxable account, especially since you're limited by how much you can contribute and when you can access the money.

Stocks and low-turnover equity funds held longer than one year are also appropriate for taxable accounts. That's because they receive preferential capital gains tax treatment compared with short-term gains or ordinary income.

### Don't focus solely on tax effects

One last piece of advice: Don't make your entire investment decisions based on tax implications. The most important element of saving is to accumulate as much as possible. Seeking tax efficiency should never impede the goal of maximizing your savings.

**The best of both tax worlds**

The previous chapter included a lot of material regarding the unknowns of the world. I advised you to make life insurance an essential part of your financial assets to help deal with those unknowns.

As I continue this chapter I'm going to take that instruction a step further. One of the best ways to prepare for whatever the world brings is to have life insurance for your whole life.

In other words, you should strongly consider investing in a permanent life insurance policy that does not expire as long as you pay the required premiums.

The most common example of a permanent life insurance policy is whole life insurance.

## WHAT IS WHOLE LIFE INSURANCE?

Whole life insurance does not expire like a term policy does. You can keep your coverage, with the same premium payment, for as long as you want or need it, without ever again going through the application or underwriting process.

Its main benefit is the lifetime guarantee. Buy whole life today and no matter how much your health changes, you can provide a death benefit to surviving beneficiaries for as long as you pay your premium.

Whole life insurance is guaranteed to remain active for your *whole life* — provided you don't allow it to lapse, as I wrote about in the previous chapter.

Your lifetime level premium amount is established when you apply for coverage. It won't increase or decrease. Today's $225 a month payment will still be $225 in 10 years, 20 years, and for the rest of your life as long as you make those payments.

That amount is established based on your risk factors, also taking into account the expenses the insurance company has.

## WHOLE LIFE INSURANCE CASH VALUE

In the first years of your policy, the insurance company has fewer expenses because you're less likely to die and because costs for everything rise over time due to inflation.

One of the benefits of whole life insurance is that the premium amount stays level for as long as you own the policy. The insurance company, therefore, sets up the payment amount so that you pay the same amount for the life of the contract, even though its expenses increase the longer you hold onto the policy.

It's similar to how your mortgage is set up, only in reverse. If you get a 30 year mortgage, the lender sets up your principal and interest payment to remain the same each month for 30 years. However, in the early years, you pay more in interest and less in principal. The longer the mortgage goes, the more principal your monthly payment covers.

The life insurance company doesn't need all of your whole life premium dollars at the beginning of the contract to cover its costs. Taking the example from above of a $225 premium, the insurance company's early-year expenses may only be $125.

The extra $100 you pay in the early years gets sets aside for later and earns interest. That's what cash value is. In the later policy years, whatever has accumulated pays for the higher expenses that your premium no longer does.

Collecting excess premium early on also enables the insurance company to recoup as much of its expenses before you pass away or surrender the policy.

**The cash value is also for your benefit**

The cash value inside a whole life insurance policy isn't just for the insurance company. If you're the owner of the policy, you can access it as well simply by withdrawing it.

Some of the common uses for using the cash value of a whole life policy are:

- Helping to pay tuition and fees for children's college
- Making a downpayment on a home
- Making home improvements
- Retirement income

Some people use the policy's cash value to pay for their premiums or to purchase additional coverage.

You can also cash out the policy at any time. When you do that, the insurance company pays you the policy's cash value minus any remaining fees and charges. Cashing out a whole life policy, known as surrendering your policy, means you no longer have life insurance coverage. Your premium requirements stop.

## TAX-ADVANTAGED GROWTH

Whole life insurance offers favorable tax treatment compared with other interest-bearing accounts. Cash value grows tax-deferred, which means there is no tax owed during the period when the money is growing inside the policy. This helps money grow faster because it's not being reduced by taxes each year and the interest you earn is on a higher amount.

Policy loans and withdrawals are also tax-free to you, the owner, and the death benefit is tax-free to your beneficiaries.

### You may receive tax-free dividends

Many life insurance companies that sell whole life will pay dividends to policyholders.

Dividends are one of the benefits of owning a whole life policy with a mutual life insurance company. Mutual insurers are those that are owned by their policyholders, not by shareholders.

As I mentioned, many whole life policies entitle owners to dividend payments based on the insurance company's earnings. That's because not only are you a policy owner, but your policy also makes you a small owner in the company itself. Policies that are set up like this are called participating policies.

The dividends from a whole life policy are generally not taxed because the IRS considers them a return of the premium you have already paid.

Tax-free dividends are another way you can build greater cash value within your whole life policy.

## Tax-free loans and withdrawals

Life insurers allow you to borrow money from your policy's cash value, up to a maximum percentage of the account value. Even if you never intend to pay the money back — meaning you're basically just doing a straight withdrawal — insurance companies consider that transaction a loan.

But because loans are generally intended to be repaid, it's not considered income and is therefore not taxable. It's not much different than obtaining a student loan, a home equity loan or a car loan. Since the intention is to repay the money with interest, the IRS does not consider the loaned funds as income.

The difference with life insurance policies is that the insurance company doesn't set a timeframe for repaying your policy. That's because they don't need the money. The insurance company wouldn't let you pull money out — at least not without a penalty — unless it had covered its costs. And if the insurer hasn't covered its costs, you wouldn't have policy cash value to withdraw anyway.

When you withdraw accumulated cash value, the insurance company lowers the policy's death benefit based on how much you pulled out. This is essentially where you pay the "tax" on withdrawals.

Many people, especially those in their 40s and 50s, buy cash value policies for the purpose of using that cash value for supplemental retirement income. When it comes time to retire, each withdrawal, whether monthly, quarterly, or annually, is treated like a policy loan even if the retiree will never repay it. As a loan, it's tax-free. Those withdrawals are also lowering the policy's death benefit, which is in essence how they are repaying the policy "loan."

One of the main advantages of borrowing against a life insurance policy instead of through traditional means is that you don't have to qualify for a policy loan. There are no credit checks to pass and no collateral to securitize the loan.

What if you want to repay your policy to re-establish the full death benefit? The good news is policies typically charge a more favorable interest rate than traditional lenders. Insurance companies can do this because they aren't trying to profit from lending money. Plus, loaned funds continue to *earn interest* as though they're still contained within the policy.

Something to keep in mind is that a policy loan is not a withdrawal from an account that you own. You're basically borrowing money from the life insurance company and using your policy as collateral.

If you pass away with an outstanding policy loan, your beneficiaries will receive a lower death benefit than if you had not withdrawn funds from the policy.

In addition to lowering the policy's death benefit, another potential downside to a life insurance policy loan is the possibility of borrowing too much out of the policy.

The cash value component of a permanent life policy is what supports the policy; it's how the various fees, mortality charges and the cost of insurance are paid. If you withdraw too much of the cash value, there won't be enough to pay those fees and you could lose all of the life insurance coverage.

If that happens, it could also trigger a taxable event. This happens because you will have essentially collected tax-free income without paying it back because there is no longer a policy to repay it to.

### Fewer restrictions on whole life

One of the advantages that whole life insurance has over tax-advantaged accounts like 401(k)s is there are no annual IRS contribution limits.

In 2023, the IRS allowed individuals to contribute a maximum of $22,500 to their 401(k) plan, up to $30,000 for people 50 and older. The IRA contribution limit was $6,500 per individual, $7,500 for people 50 and older. If you could afford to contribute more to one of these retirement plans, you still couldn't.

Life insurance doesn't have this restriction. It should be noted that there are some limits, but they are not as restrictive as what the IRS imposes on retirement accounts.

One restriction is that life insurers can't allow you to have more coverage than what is suitable for your situation. This means they can't sell you, say, a $10 million life insurance policy if you earn less than $100,000 a year.

There is also is a maximum amount of premium you can put into a policy at a time for it to still qualify as a life insurance contract.

To build cash value quicker, many policyholders will pay more in premium than what the contract requires. This is perfectly legal, up to a point.

A maximum is established by the IRS to prevent people from stuffing money into an insurance policy to take advantage of the tax-free interest growth. Basically, you can't buy $50,000 in coverage and pay $25,000 in annual premium just to build greater tax-free cash value.

Another way whole life insurance is less restrictive than tax advantaged accounts is that you don't have to wait until age 59 1/2 to access your money, nor are you required to use it only for retirement. Life insurance cash value can be accessed at any time, so long as the policy has enough cash value to support the coverage. Plus, you can use those funds for any purpose you choose.

## Chapter 3 summary

Life insurance has immense potential as a tool for creating tax-free financial abundance. By understanding and utilizing its unique tax benefits and growth mechanics, you can unlock a wealth-building strategy that not only protects your loved ones but also maximizes their financial prosperity.

Now that you have a better understanding of whole life insurance's tax advantages, as well as the benefits of policy loans, Chapter 4 will delve deeper into the potential of life insurance as a powerful tool for building lasting wealth and achieving financial abundance.

# FOSTERING WEALTH ACCUMULATION THROUGH LIFE INSURANCE

---

*"The basic purpose of life insurance is to create cash...nothing more or nothing less. Everything else confuses and complicates."*

— BEN FELDMAN

---

Have you ever been to Disneyland? Or eaten at McDonald's? Shopped at JCPenney?

If so, you partially owe that experience to the value and versatility of permanent, cash value life insurance.

But decades before these iconic businesses were supported by their founders' use of cash value life insurance, one of the most prestigious universities in the United States stayed afloat during hard times thanks to life insurance proceeds.

## HOW LIFE INSURANCE SAVED STANFORD UNIVERSITY

LeLand Stanford was the first president of Pacific Mutual Life, known today as Pacific Life. He was also the owner of the first policy issued by the company in 1868.

Stanford and his wife, Jane, lost their 15-year-old son LeLand Jr. to typhoid in 1884. This tragedy prompted the couple to invest in higher education, and they opened Stanford University in 1891.

Tragedy struck again in 1893 when the elder LeLand Stanford passed away. But that policy issued to LeLand by Pacific Mutual 25 years earlier came to the rescue. Jane used the policy proceeds to keep the university operating, including paying faculty. This allowed Stanford to stay open during the immediate years after its co-founder's death, when financial support from other sources was uncertain.

## HOW OTHER ICONIC BRANDS BENEFITTED FROM LIFE INSURANCE

Fast forward a few years to the year 1898. James Cash Penney was invited to joined a retail partnership. Less than 10 years later, he bought out his partners and rebranded the retail business as JCPenney. By 1929, he owned 1,400 stores across the U.S.

Most people know what happened in 1929. The stock market crashed, ushering the Great Depression. As with most businesses of that era, JCPenney struggled. But its owner kept it afloat by borrowing from his cash value life insurance policy to make payroll and cover expenses until the economy turned around. Though the chain has fewer stores today than it did in 1929, it's still a vibrant part of the nation's retail landscape.

In the 1950s, two of the country's most iconic brands were born thanks to cash value life insurance.

Walt Disney, having started a successful animation studio decades earlier, wanted to open an amusement park. But he couldn't find anybody to finance or invest in the idea. Undeterred, Disney sold one of his homes and borrowed against his life insurance policy. He used those funds to pay employees of the animation studios, who worked on developing the park idea to the point it was able to obtain financing. Disneyland opened in 1955 and is today one of 12 theme parks the company operates around the world.

That same year, Ray Kroc opened his first McDonald's franchise restaurant in Illinois. Six years later, he bought out the original McDonald's brothers in California. As with many new businesses, those initial years were a struggle. Kroc stayed afloat partly through borrowing from two cash value life insurance policies to cover salaries of key employees. Today, the world's largest restaurant chain has about 30,000 locations.

Though not all entrepreneurs become as famous as these examples, many have taken advantage of the value and versatility of cash value life insurance to provide startup capital or operating expenses during lean years of their companies.

**If it's a good idea to them, why not for you?**

This chapter covers how life insurance can help you create lasting wealth and achieve financial abundance.

I led this chapter with the above stories for a few reasons. One, these are real-life examples of how smart people used life insurance at a time of need and uncertainty.

Second, the attributes of cash value life insurance that make it a valuable resource for entrepreneurs can also make it a viable resource for you and your family.

Also, these examples show that the strategies I'm writing about in this book are not new, untested concepts. Again, very successful people have employed these strategies for decades.

The reason they're not used by more people, or why you may have never heard of these concepts, is like a lot of aspects of our capitalist economy: The best ideas and the best advice are almost exclusively available to the upper class. They rarely trickle down to the middle class, the working class, the Proletariat. If they are talked about, it's often in a tone of voice designed to scare you away from the idea of buying permanent life insurance.

I'm one of the people hoping to change that. Because everybody deserves the opportunity to build wealth and to transfer as much of it as they can to future generations.

## A LOT OF WEALTH IS ABOUT TO BE TRANSFERRED

That's one of the major themes of this book. And for good reason.

It is anticipated that an incredible amount of wealth will continue to be transferred to younger generations between now and the year 2045. Estimates of what Baby Boomers and a handful of older generation households will bequeath directly to their heirs range between $68 trillion and $75 trillion during this unprecedented period.

This book aims to not only help make this transfer as efficient as possible for the current generations, but also to help those beneficiaries maintain and grow the wealth they inherit. That way, they can also transfer as much as possible to future generations.

I'm also making the case in this book that the greatest tool to accomplish both objectives is life insurance.

## MAKING SURE WEALTH GOES TO THOSE WHO MATTER TO YOU

One of the goals most families have when leaving an inheritance is to ensure those beneficiaries receive as much as possible. That's not to suggest people hoard their money or limit their spending while living to give as much away as possible.

What it does mean is that when people who have spent their lives creating wealth pass away, they would rather it go to people who matter to them: their children, grandchildren, charitable organizations and others who enhanced their lives.

They do not want a significant part of their estate going to lawyers, health care providers and — especially — the IRS.

Proper planning, including the purchase of the right life insurance coverage, can help people accomplish these goals. It can help ensure wealth lasts for generations and makes a difference to those who matter the most.

When I write about using life insurance for wealth accumulation and as an inheritance tool, I'm referring to permanent life insurance, rather than term insurance. The latter may have a place in your financial planning. But by and large, the planning strategies discussed in this book require permanent coverage you can count on for the duration of your life.

That's because permanent insurance can fulfill two financial goals that term insurance cannot guarantee because of its temporary nature and lack of cash value. Permanent cash value life insurance can:

- Potentially provide income replacement and a source of needed funds during one's living years (i.e. "living benefits")
- Potentially provide a means to guarantee long-term family wealth after one's death by providing a death benefit.

What's more, you can execute these wealth building and transfer strategies using whole life insurance, the most common form of permanent life coverage. There are several other types of permanent coverage you could use, depending on your circumstances. I will touch upon other types of permanent life insurance later in this chapter.

## LEVERAGING YOUR PREMIUM DOLLARS

One of the benefits of using permanent life insurance is the ability to leverage your premium dollars.

One of the criticisms of buying permanent life insurance is the cost. People who suggest you should only ever buy term life believe that the potential benefits of permanent life insurance do not outweigh the much greater cost of the coverage.

What these naysayers omit in their criticism is the positive return on the investment that you and/or your beneficiaries are nearly guaranteed to earn from this investment over time.

Here's a real-world comparison of the difference between term and permanent life insurance: If term life insurance is like renting your home, then permanent life insurance is akin to buying a house.

When you rent, you pay money each month for the privilege of living in the home. You receive nothing in return. You have zero ownership rights in the property. When it's time to move, you're lucky to collect the security deposit back that you paid when you first moved in.

When you buy a home, it may cost more than renting. In addition to paying your mortgage lender interest on a loan, there are also insurance, property taxes and maintenance to consider.

But with each mortgage payment, as well as the increase in your home's value, you're creating what's called equity. This is the difference between the home's value and what you still owe on the mortgage loan.

Home equity is similar to a life insurance policy's cash value in that you can access it for other financial needs. Plus, when you sell your home, whatever equity you had built up in the property — minus the expenses of selling a home — are your's to take with you.

## HERE'S WHY IT'S WORTH PAYING MORE

Here's how whole life insurance naysayers try to convince not to invest in permanent life insurance.

A popular life insurance rate website indicates that a 30-year-old man in generally good health will pay about $920 a month for a $1 million whole life insurance policy. The same man could buy a $1 million 30-year term life insurance for about $80 a month.

Why, you might be asking, should I pay nearly 12 times more money each month for the same amount of coverage?

Here's why: The permanent life insurance policy is guaranteed to provide you and/or your beneficiaries a positive return on your investment. The term policy is not.

Let me explain. As long as you pay that $920 in premium every month, the whole life policy is guaranteed to pay a death benefit. What's more, it's a virtual certainty that the death benefit will pay out more ($1 million) than the premiums you will have paid over the life of the policy.

In fact, it would take more than *90 years* for you to spend $1 million on premiums, at which point the 30-year-old man would be 120 years old.

Even if you defy current science and actually live to 120, you won't be paying premiums that long. In this scenario, the whole life insurance policy is considered "paid up" at age 100. That means once you reach 100, the insurance company no longer requires premium payments. This is how most whole life policies work. If this person were to live to 105, 110 or 120, they're guaranteed to have a $1 million death benefit — provided they haven't used the cash value — without paying additional premium past age 100.

If that were to happen to this 30-year-old, he would have paid $772,800 in premium over 70 years to generate a $1 million death benefit. That's a 29 percent return on the investment. The return is greater if this man dies sooner (not that I'm suggesting he do that, just pointing it out).

Now let's compare that to the 30-year-old who bought 30-year term. At age 60, relatively young in this age of increasing longevity, the man will essentially lose his coverage, though he can possibly get more at a much higher rate. Over 30 years, he will have paid $28,800 in premium — and received nothing in return. No cash value, no death benefit. Just like the home renter.

Yes, the whole life policy owner paid more, but he could have had coverage for 40 additional years — or more — beyond what the term life policy holder did.

Yes, the whole life policy owner paid more, but he is all but guaranteed to leave that $1 million to his heirs when he dies, assuming he didn't withdraw its cash value; the term life policy holder is not.

Yes, the whole life policy owner paid more, but if he decided at any point that he didn't need coverage, he gets to keep every penny that's accumulated — minus any remaining charges owed to the insurance company. Just like the homeowner who sells their property. The term life policy holder on the other hand, will not get anything if their coverage expires or is surrendered.

Yes, the whole life policy owner paid more, but he had cash value to help fortify his finances, like when his kids started college, or he wanted to buy a vacation home, or he was hospitalized after having heart surgery. The term life insurance policy holder never had $1 of cash value to draw upon.

## THERE ARE OTHER BENEFITS ALSO

Permanent life insurance offers additional benefits as a wealth transfer and inheritance tool. Some of these I may have already covered; some I may yet again. But these are really important concepts and can't be overstated.

**Simplicity**: Permanent life insurance is fairly straightforward, especially compared with the complexity of other financial tools and investments.

**Tax benefits**: I covered these in detail in the last chapter, but just a quick refresher: You can access the policy's cash value tax-free in most circumstances and the death benefit to your beneficiaries is tax-free as well.

**Probate avoidance**. Probate is the process of distributing a decedent's assets upon their death, which includes administering the person's will if one existed. This is often a complicated, lengthy, arduous — though legally necessary — process. The good news with life insurance is that the proceeds go directly to the named beneficiaries without being part of the probate process.

**Creditor exemption**. Depending on your state of residence, life insurance death benefits may be exempt from claims that creditors have against the policyholder. This means beneficiaries wouldn't be forced to pay those creditors with the policy proceeds. In addition, beneficiaries that have outstanding claims against them typically do not have to hand over life insurance proceeds they receive. Also, creditors typically cannot force you to access your policy's cash value to pay debts, though you certainly can do so voluntarily if it would help you in the long run.

## THE BENEFIT OF BEING YOUR OWN LENDER

At the beginning of the chapter, I mentioned that the attributes of cash value life insurance that make it a valuable resource for entrepreneurs can also make it a viable resource for you and your family.

Here are those attributes:

**Liquidity**. Cash flow is the lifeblood of any business. Money should always be flowing into a business so that it can pay for operations, payroll and large one-time expenses like equipment. Some businesses, by nature, can't always count on regular influxes of cash, either because of the seasonality of their businesses or because they need money to do the actual work before they get paid for it.

Families and households need cash too. You may have unexpected, unbudgeted bills or expenses arise. You may find yourself out of work or unable to work. When these situations arise, you can access funds in short order with a call to the insurance company or by filling out a short form. Life insurance cash value is almost as accessible as money you keep in a bank savings account.

**You don't have to qualify or provide collateral.** Applying for traditional financing typically means filling out an application and undergoing a credit check to assess your ability to repay the loan. If your credit isn't so good, lenders may charge you a higher interest rate or deny funding altogether. Lenders typically make you put up something of value to secure the loan in case you can't pay. Your life insurance policy doesn't require any of this. You want money, it's yours.

**There's little to no interest charged**. If you borrow from a traditional lender — or an unscrupulous one — they will charge you interest on what you borrow. Life insurance companies do charge interest on policy loans, but it's typically lower than what traditional lenders charge. Also, the life insurance company doesn't even require you to repay the money; if you choose you can just have the insurer lower the policy's death benefit in exchange for the withdrawn funds.

**There's so specific timetable for repayment**. Like I just wrote, there's no mandate to repaying a life insurance policy loan. If you want to, you can take as long as you need to put the money back, varying the size and frequency of those payments along the way. Lenders want a specific amount of money each month until the loan is paid in full, and they typically dictate how long you have to do that. It's helpful for businesses not to have a rigid repayment schedule when borrowing money, just like it would be for you and your household.

**Safe growth**. Cash value inside a life insurance policy is credited interest and accumulates in value. And, with exception (see the end of the chapter), all permanent life insurance policies grow without any exposure to the stock market or other risky investments that often lose value.

Running a business is risky enough; entrepreneurs can't risk their liquid assets on investments that can deplete their reserves. Likewise, families and households need a source of funds they can count on being available without worrying about the whims of the stock market.

## SPEAKING OF GROWTH: LET'S DISCUSS RETURNS

Businesses frequently analyze, measure and discuss returns. You've probably heard the term as well, but how well do you understand its meaning?

I want you to understand it as much as possible. Because if you're looking to build wealth and transfer as much of it as possible to future generations, you need to understand how to maximize returns on that wealth.

### What is a return?

The general term is simple to understand. A return is how much money one either makes or loses on an investment.

If you invest $100 and it grows to $110 at the end of the first year, you generated an annual return of 10 percent. If that $100 falls in value to $90 after the first year, you suffered a negative 10 percent return.

Returns can be measured for any length of time. Annually seems to be the most used. This makes it easier to compare one year to the next. People often calculate a holding return, which is the profit or loss generated during the total amount of time an asset has been held. For example, if you bought real estate five years ago that is worth 10 percent more today, the 5-year holding return would be 10 percent.

Returns can be expressed as the nominal change in dollar value of an investment (My investment in this asset generated a $100 return), or as a percentage change (My investment generated a 25 percent return).

**Real return vs nominal return**

When it comes to considering life insurance as an investment and an asset, it's important to be more specific about what your return is. This is especially true if you want to compare the returns on life insurance with other asset classes.

To get a clear picture of life insurance returns, you should use a real rate of return.

The real rate of return is defined as the return on an asset that's been adjusted for outside impacts to the value of the investment. These include inflation, taxes and fees you pay to buy and hold the investment.

The real rate of return will typically be lower than the nominal rate of return, which calculates a return based solely on the movement of the investment's value without factoring for taxes, inflation or other adjustments.

Why is a real rate of return important? As I wrote in the previous chapter, investments and asset classes have different tax treatments. Some are taxed in full. Others are tax-deferred. Life insurance, in most cases, is not taxed at all.

Therefore, if you want to understand whether a taxable investment provides a better, worse, or same rate of return as a tax-free investment, you need a real rate of return that considers the cost of taxes. The same holds true if you're comparing assets that charge different fee schedules.

For example, investment in a stock mutual fund might have a better nominal rate of return than a whole life insurance policy. This means its overall value before taxes and fees will likely be higher.

But factoring in taxes and fees in calculating a return might give the whole life policy a better real rate of return than the mutual fund, or at the very least make it more competitive. After all, mutual funds are subject to capital gains taxes, where life insurance is generally tax-free. They have different fees and expenses, as well.

The real rate of return is important because it calculates how much money you really have after you've paid taxes and fees on an investment.

**Real return vs real return**

Another way for businesses and households to use the real rate of return is to calculate the return on an investment that was financed by cash value life insurance against the same investment financed by credit or traditional lending.

In this scenario, you simply factor in the interest and fees charged when borrowing money, both from the policy and from other sources. Obviously, the less you pay in interest and fees to finance an investment or purchase, the greater your rate of return.

## CONSIDER THE RISKS WHEN EVALUATING RETURNS

Everybody who invests has a risk tolerance. Some are willing to handle more risk while others don't have the leeway — or the stomach — to risk their money on something that could lose value over time.

Regardless of where you fall, the more risk you take, the higher potential return you expect to earn. Likewise, if you don't want any risk, you should never anticipate a high return. The better returns are the tradeoff to compensate investors for taking more risk while lower returns are the tradeoff for knowing you likely won't lose money.

Therefore, if you're investing in a risky stock, like a company based in an unstable country that is doing cutting-edge technology, you expect there to at least be the potential for a large return on that investment. You might even hope to double your money in the short term. On the other hand, if research indicated the highest potential return is only 5 percent, you'd be foolish to invest.

By contrast, life insurance offers nearly risk-free investing because it's mostly insulated from various market and economic risks. Insurance companies must legally have stable finances and management to do business, so the risk of these companies defaulting on their obligations is minimal. Given the lack of risk in buying life insurance, it would be unreasonable to expect 15 to 20 percent or higher annual returns.

## OTHER TYPES OF PERMANENT LIFE INSURANCE CAN CARRY A LITTLE MORE RISK

So far, I've mostly covered whole life insurance. However, there are other types of permanent coverage you may consider when executing the strategies in this book, depending on your individual situation.

**Universal life insurance.** Universal life (UL) can also cover an individual for his or her entire life, though it's not as simple or straightforward as whole life. UL is also the more expensive option between the two.

Universal life policies typically do not offer a level premium payment. Instead, it's the policy owner's responsibility to pay adequate premium over the life of the policy to support the life insurance coverage.

Your UL premium goes into the policy's account value. The insurance company takes what it needs to cover its costs. Any amount remaining is the policy's cash value. As with whole life, the insurance company will pay interest on the cash value.

One of the main differences between UL and whole life is that UL premiums and death benefits do not remain level like they do with whole life. Both amounts can vary. What will largely determine how much you will pay and the benefit your policy pays is the interest your policy's cash value earns.

The more interest credited to your policy, the more cash value it accumulates, and the higher your death benefit. Higher cash values also mean that you can reduce your premium payment and still maintain your coverage.

On the flip side, your policy could lapse if the cash value doesn't earn sufficient interest to cover policy charges. Some policy owners have to increase their premium payments during periods when the policy earns less interest than projected.

There are basically three types of UL policies that differ based on how interest is credited to the policy's cash value:

- Fixed UL polices offer a fixed rate set by the insurance company that is based largely on the economic climate. In other words, if interest rates in the overall economy are high, fixed UL policies will earn higher interest; and vice versa.
- Variable UL policies are the closest thing to a traditional investment in the world of life insurance. Policy owners select investment accounts that are similar to mutual funds in which to invest their cash value. This puts your insurance coverage at the greatest risk of any other type of policy. If those accounts decline in value, as investments often do, your cash value will decrease. Since the policy needs that cash value to stay active, you could lose your coverage without making enough premium payments to cover those investment losses. If your investments perform well, your cash value will grow faster than it would with a fixed UL.
- Indexed UL is marketed by insurance companies as combining the investment returns of variable UL with

the risk profile of fixed UL. Interest is earned based on a market index, such as the S&P 500. But your cash value isn't invested in the index or any investment funds. The index is merely a measuring stick. That allows the insurance company to protect the policy's cash value from losing money if the corresponding index loses value: Your cash value just remains the same if that happens. The shield from market losses is offset by a cap the insurer applies on interest growth.

Universal life's key benefit is its flexibility. You're not obligated to pay the same premium amount every month; you can vary them as long as you maintain enough cash value. Accumulating a certain amount of cash value can actually increase your death benefit.

The potential negatives of UL are its cost and complexity. Because of these traits, it's easier to lapse a UL policy than it is a whole life policy.

**Life insurance with long-term care benefits**. Many insurance carriers offer hybrid long-term care insurance. This is a policy that combines long-term care insurance with life insurance.

Many life insurance policies have optional long-term care riders that pay monthly benefit to cover the cost of a nursing home or other long-term care facility. Those funds are deducted from the policy's death benefit; it's another example of the "living benefits" many life insurance policies offer.

**Survivorship life insurance.** This is a single policy that insures two people. It's also known as second-to-die insurance. The death benefit is paid when the second insured person dies.

Survivorship policies were originally created for estate planning at a time when estate tax laws changed to exempt a surviving spouse from paying the tax on the deceased spouse's share of the estate. The policy's death benefit kicks in when both insureds pass away to help cover estate tax obligations that the estate's heirs would owe.

This is especially helpful if a couple's estate is comprised mostly of non-liquid assets like a business, farm, real estate, artwork, automobile collection or other valuable items. The policy would be designed to cover the estate tax to avoid having to sell non-liquid assets.

Similarly, if a couple has a large 401(k), IRA or other qualified plan, a non-spouse beneficiary of that fund will owe income taxes upon receiving that money. A survivorship life insurance policy can provide enough money to pay the income tax.

Survivorship life is commonly used in complex transferring of business interests and real estate to non-spouses where assets may have to be split for fairness, or if the insureds want to include a charity in their estate transfer.

Couples with a child who has special needs sometimes use survivorship policies to fund the child's care expenses in the event they both pass away before the child.

**Guaranteed issue life insurance.** As its name implies, a guaranteed issue policy provides automatic life insurance coverage to those who apply. You won't be turned down because of underwriting factors, because there is no underwriting, though some guaranteed issue policies may disqualify an application using knockout questions related to the possibility of immediate terminal illnesses.

Once issued, these policies are guaranteed to provide a death benefit as long as you pay the required premiums.

Because of the risk to the insurance company and guarantees involved, these policies limit the amount of coverage you can own, usually to a cap of $25,000. They are mostly designed to help older individuals provide a death benefit to cover funeral costs and any estate settlement expenses.

Guaranteed issue policies won't help much with the wealth transfer strategies offered in this book. However, because of the ease in getting coverage, if you're an older individual it may not hurt to have a little extra to cover funeral costs, leaving your other life insurance coverage for other financial goals.

**Single-premium life insurance.** This is a rarely used type of life insurance in which the policy owners pays a single, lump-sum payment to purchase a permanent policy. There are no ongoing premiums once that payment is made.

This type of policy is typically used by older people to create a larger legacy, using large sums of money they don't think they'll need in the future. For example, a widow who receives a death benefit from a deceased spouse who doesn't need those funds to live can buy a single-premium life insurance policy and name children or grandchildren as beneficiaries. Funds sitting in dormant accounts such as annuities or CDs are also a potential source of funds for a single-premium policy.

One of the downsides of this approach is that your tax-free access to the policy's cash value is limited. That's because a large premium payment modifies the policy to the point where it no longer meets the IRS definition of life insurance; it's essentially a taxable account that has instantly generated taxable interest if withdrawn. This is known as a modified endowment contract (MEC).

However, the death benefit will in most cases pass to beneficiaries tax-free, just as with other types of life insurance.

---

**Chapter 4 summary**

The goal of this chapter was to explain the need for cash, whether you're a business or you're looking to create and accumulate wealth. For decades, many entrepreneurs and families have used cash value life insurance, primarily whole life insurance, to build cash reserves that they have tapped in times when they needed immediate cash flow with no hassles and no penalties. In most recent decades, the insurance industry has created other forms of life insurance that can assist with cash accumulation and wealth building.

Next up is Chapter 5, in which I will cover the many types of investment risks and where permanent life insurance fits in the risk spectrum.

# Rising Above the Jargon

*"When getting help with money, whether it is insurance, real estate or investments you should always look for a person with the heart of a teacher, not the heart of a salesman."*

— DAVE RAMSEY

Let's be honest, life insurance isn't the first thing most people think of when they're looking to build their wealth. We tend to think of it as expensive and complicated, possibly a scam designed to get us to part with our money, and probably not something we need if we're healthy and have no dependents. As you're discovering now, these are myths, and they're what stand in the way of most people realizing just how much of an asset life insurance really is.

For those who do have an inkling that this should be something they find out more about, the jargon is off-putting, and many people put the brakes on before they even have any idea what the path looks like.

This book marks my intention to change that. I want to help as many people as I can to develop their wealth in a way that's both tax-efficient and easy to work with no matter what the economy looks like.

My goal now is to make sure all those people who are looking for this information have access to it – and find it before they find a ton of daunting insurance lingo that puts them off before they even start. And for that, I need your help – but don't worry, it won't take more than a few minutes.

**By leaving a review of this book on Amazon, you'll show other people who are looking for this knowledge exactly where they can find it presented in a clear and concise way – so they can start making progress as quickly as possible.**

Simply by letting other readers know how this book has helped you and what they can find inside, you'll make sure they find what they're looking for.

Thank you so much for your support. To make information powerful, we have to make sure we share it.

# RISK REALITIES: ASSESSING LIFE INSURANCE

*"It's not whether you're right or wrong that's important, but how much money you make when you're right and how much you lose when you're wrong."*

— GEORGE SOROS

M any of the decisions we make in life involve risk. In return, they should also offer the potential for reward.

Let's say you want to ask out a person you've had a crush on for awhile. There's always the risk they'll say no. Or you might find out later they're not the person they appeared to be from afar.

One potential reward is you both live happily ever after.

You take a risk every time you apply for a job, buy a car, or try a new restaurant. But if you don't take the risk, you'll never experience the rewards those decisions might provide.

## THE MULTITUDE OF INVESTMENT RISKS

Perhaps nowhere do we understand the dichotomy of risk and reward than in how we invest money.

Every investment involves some level of risk to varying degrees. There are extreme risks like cryptocurrency or buying into a brand new company. On the opposite end are savings accounts in banks and U.S. savings bonds.

The extreme risks promise the potential for higher returns with a corresponding risk that you'll lose your entire investment. The safer options promise a little growth, but greater peace of mind.

Even the safest option for "investing" your money — burying cash in your back yard or stuffing it in a cookie jar — carries risk. No, I'm not saying vermin might come along and eat your cash.

But there's a risk that the $100 you bury will be worth much less when you dig it up.

This is called "inflation risk," and it's just one of many risks involved when we invest and manage our finances.

We call these "market risks" or "investment risks." This is a term used to refer to the specific risks you take on when you invest — or even if you choose never to invest — your money. Market risks involve the many possibilities defined by the behaviors and movements of the various investment markets and the economy in general.

There is a level of uncertainty involved in every decision: the job offer, the car, the restaurant, and especially your money. Uncertainty equals risk.

It's impossible to eliminate market risk entirely. You can, however, manage it to a point that you're more inclined to reach your financial goals. But first, you have to understand the many types of market risk you'll encounter, not just the the risk that your investment won't grow.

Here is an overview of the various types of market risks:

**Equity risk**

This is the type of risk most people associate with investing. It's the risk that the market price of your investment drops in value. This can happen to a wide range of investments, most notably when you buy stocks and mutual funds.

If you buy an investment at the peak of a booming market, you're taking on more equity risk than if you're buying something that recently declined in value.

**Interest rate risk**

Some investments are at risk of changes in interest rates. Interest rate risk mostly affects investments that pay a fixed rate of investments, such as bonds.

When interest rates increase, it lowers the value of bonds and fixed-rate instruments bought at a lower interest rate. That's because a bond paying a rate of, say, 5 percent, is worth more to an investor than one paying 3 percent.

The longer the duration on a fixed investment, the more sensitive it is to interest rate risk. In other words, there's more risk that a 10-year bond will drop in value due to interest rate risk than a five-year bond.

Higher interest rates can also have a detrimental affect on investments in commodities and real estate.

On the other hand, lower interest rates means you'll earn less on bank savings accounts and certificates of deposit. Lower interest rates also lower your earning potential on fixed-rate annuities.

### Liquidity risk

Liquidity risk refers to how easily you can convert an investment into cash. There may come a point where you need cash quickly. If you're invested too much in investments that have high liquidity risk, it won't be easy to sell your investments to obtain needed cash.

For example, investing in real estate often carries high liquidity risk. Much of this is due to the time it usually takes to complete the process of selling property. This risk is heightened if the market makes it tougher to unload real estate. For example, it wasn't easy to sell homes for a decent price during the financial crisis of 2007-2008. Likewise, finding buyers for office space proved arduous during and immediately after the Covid pandemic when companies were forced to institute work-from-home policies.

There's also liquidity risk in retirement plans such as 401(k)s and IRAs because they can't be accessed without a heavy tax penalty before the owner reaches age 59 1/2.

**Inflation risk**

Your investments are subject to inflation risk when they fail to generate a rate of return that is at least equal to the rate of inflation. Inflation erodes your returns and lowers the purchasing power of your money.

For example, if inflation from one year to the next is 3 percent, but your investment portfolio only generated a 2 percent return, you lost purchasing power in that year. In theory, you lost money by not earning at least a 3-percent return to keep pace with inflation.

Inflation risk is typically highest on safer, low-return investments such as CDs. Ironically, because of inflation risk, investors need to take other types of market risk to maximize their returns enough to negate the effects of inflation.

**Currency risk**

Commonly referred to as exchange-rate risk, this type of risk is incurred by investors who invest in foreign companies or assets. Currency risk relates to how one currency can become more or less valuable than another. This often creates unpredictable profits and losses for investors who live in one country but own stocks in others. A U.S. investor with shares of

Chinese companies has to keep track of not only the change in the stock price of those companies, but also in the value of the yuan, the Chinese currency. Both will affect the investor's realized return.

Currency prices fluctuate based on the level of global demand for the nation's output. High demand increases the value of a country's currency while falling demand weakens a country's currency.

Some foreign currencies carry less risk than others because of their overall stability. This is true of the Swiss franc.

**Foreign Investment risk**

This is different from currency risk, in that it covers the stability — or lack thereof — in the government and economy of a nation in which your investments are based. Wars, natural disasters, political unrest and economic collapses can and usually will have major detrimental effects on any assets based in that country, including stocks, bonds and real estate. Investments in many countries are more susceptible to this type of risk because those nations are more susceptible to destabilizing events.

**Credit risk**

Credit risk is involved when you purchase bonds. A bond is debt issued by a company or government. When you purchase a bond, you're essentially loaning the issuer money, with the promise of the return of your principal plus interest. As with any borrower, there is always the risk that a company or government defaults on the loan, denying bond holders their return. Companies and governments deemed higher risk tend to pay higher rates of interest to bond holders.

## Commodity risk

Commodities are raw materials that are either sold directly to consumers or used in construction or manufacturing. These include everything from corn to coffee to rubber to wood to precious metals.

You can invest in commodities in a number of ways. You can buy the actual raw commodity in bulk, such as gold or silver. You can also invest in futures contracts, in funds that track a commodity index, or buying shares of commodity-related businesses.

Commodity risk mostly refers to the extreme volatility in commodity prices. The price of commodities are significantly affected by world events, political environments, economic conditions, natural disasters and other factors. Because of this volatility, it's possible for commodity investments to lose value.

There's also commodity risk involved when you invest in companies that depend on commodities in doing business. Any company that depends on fuel, such as transportation, is at risk of falling profits when fuel prices rise significantly. Therefore, if you as an investor own shares in, say, an airline, your investment could fall in value due to commodity risk.

## Concentration risk

Concentration risk refers to the risk of losing the value in your investment portfolio because it's too concentrated in a single security or type of security. For example, if all or nearly all of your savings is invested in retail stocks, then a downturn in the economy that causes retail stocks to lose value will put your portfolio at greater risk than if you were more diversified.

## HOW TO ASSESS RISK

How do you know how risky a potential investment or what type of risk(s) it's susceptible to? There are a number of ways to assess risk.

### Research historical performance

Anybody who sells investments is usually required to provide some form of this disclaimer: "Past performance is no guarantee of future results."

This is true. After all, when it comes to investing, there are never 100 percent guarantees. There's always risk.

However, you can do a better job of predicting or anticipating future results by reviewing how an investment performed in the past. Here are a few trends to look for when using historical performance to assess risk:

- How volatile has the investment been; like a rollercoaster or more steady?
- What kind of returns has it generated in the past five, 10 or 20 years?
- How did it perform during times when the economy was rough, such as the 2007-2008 financial crisis or the early 2000s when the stock market cratered?

- On the flip side, how good were the returns during times of prosperity?
- Has the investment been rising so much that it may be due to lose value soon, or is it currently undervalued?

**Read analyses**

Another way to assess risk of an investment is to read what experts think about it.

Again, these experts can't predict everything 100 percent accurately. They're fallible like anyone else. They make mistakes in judgement. Unfortunately, some experts' opinion may be tainted by biases or even outright fraud.

However, if you read several sources of analysis, you have a better chance of understanding the inherent risks involved with an investment opportunity.

Here are a few sources of expert opinion and analysis you should look for:

**Analysts opinions.** There are people in the financial world whose job it is to study the ins and outs of a company or investment, then give opinions to potential investors. In the example of company stock, analysts will examine a company's operations, its products and services, its management, its competition, its strategy and a host of other factors.

These analysts often provide detailed written reports. Other times, they may offer brief opinions to investors on how much the stock price might increase or decrease, and include opinions such as "Buy," "Sell," or "Hold."

**Rating agency opinions.** Rating agencies are similar to investment analysts. The major difference is that a rating agency is more concerned with an entity's financial stability and its ability to meet its obligations than it is about whether it's a good investment.

Rating agencies such as Standard & Poor's and Fitch Ratings assess banks, insurance companies, governments and corporations that issue debt, and other entities for their likelihood of meeting current and future obligations to depositors, bond holders, and policyholders.

Agencies conduct independent examinations of an entity's financial health to determine its rating. Once they've done a full evaluation, the agencies assign a letter grade. Just like in school, higher letter grades indicate better performance — in this case, financial performance.

**Prospectus:** Most types of investments, especially stocks, bonds, and mutual funds, are required by law to provide potential investors with a prospectus. This is a report detailing what the investment is, what its financials look like and even the risks associated with that investment. For example, if you were to invest in the stock of a company, you can find out what the company's management thinks are its main risks. A mutual fund prospectus will inform you what types of securities it invests in and its overall investment strategy.

**Quarterly and annual reports**. Companies that have issued public stock are also required to provide detailed reports on a quarterly and/or annual basis. A company's quarterly and annual reports, for example, will provide the public with information on how much money the company made or lost, how much it currently owns in assets and how much it owes in liabilities.

**Media reports**. Though not as detailed as the aforementioned examples, media reports can provide a decent amount of information about a potential investment. You can glean the opinions of multiple sources from an article or blog, plus analysis of the overall economy and whether it may pose an increased or decreased risk to the investment in question.

**Measure using statistical analysis**

A more involved method of measuring risk is to use statistical analysis. You'll need to know some above-basic math — or find somebody who does — to use these methods of risk assessment.

Using statistical analysis can help you determine an investment's return compared to its risk. This, in turn, can help you determine whether the potential return is worth the risk involved with the investment.

Here are the most common measurements of risk:

**Standard deviation**. In math, this is a way of measuring how much data is scattered or distributed away from its expected — or standard — value. With investments, using standard deviation is a way of measuring an investment's volatility, which in turn indicates risk. An investment with a high standard deviation experiences higher volatility and is therefore considered a riskier investment.

**Sharpe ratio.** This is a way to analyze whether an investment's return is worth the associated risk. It's calculated by removing the risk-free rate of return from the overall expected return on an investment, then dividing that number by the investment's standard deviation. This ratio is often used to compare different investments; for example, one can use it to understand which companies or industries generate higher returns for a given level of risk.

**Beta.** This is a way to measure risk of a security or sector compared with the entire stock market. If you take the entire stock market and give it a beta value of one, a security with a beta greater than one is more volatile — and thus, more risky — than the market as a whole. A beta of less than one means less volatility and less risk.

**Value at Risk (VaR).** This measures the maximum potential loss for a portfolio or company during a specified period. For example, if a portfolio of investments has a 15 percent chance of losing $1 million in value in one year, the portfolio would be said to have a one-year 15-percent VaR of $1 million. VaR is most useful when assessing the likelihood of a specific outcome occurring.

The higher the chances of a higher amount of potential loss over a shorter period of time, the riskier the investment. For example, consider three investments with the following VaR:

1. One year 15% VaR of $1 million
2. One year 25% VaR of $5 million
3. Two year 5% VaR of $1 million

No. 2 is a much riskier investment than No. 1 because the odds of losing money are greater, and the potential loss is greater over the same one-year period.

But No. 3 is less risky than No. 1 because there's less chance of losing money over a two-year period than there is of losing it over one year.

Calculating a VaR can be done using historical data. More complicated calculations require higher degrees of math skills.

**R-squared.** This measurement assesses risk by comparing a fund or security to a benchmark index. The higher the R-square value, the more that independent variables are causing movement in the value of a fund or security. This makes it more risky because changes in value can't be attributed as much to macro causes like the overall economy or events that affect an entire sector.

## HOW TO MANAGE INVESTMENT RISK

When investing, you can't avoid risk. Even if you keep everything in cash stashed inside the walls of your home, you're taking on risk because that money could be stolen or burned in a fire. And as I mentioned before, you're definitely increasing your inflation risk by not generating enough returns to keep up with the higher prices of goods and services caused by inflation.

While you can't avoid investment risk, you can manage it. Here are the most common methods:

## Determine your risk tolerance

Effectively managing risk first requires you to understand how much risk you can handle. Risk tolerance includes your ability to both financially and psychologically handle potential losses in parts of your investment portfolio.

If you can weather some losses without losing sleep or your shirt, you probably have a higher risk tolerance. But your risk tolerance is low if every piece of bad news has your stomach churning and if temporary losses mean borrowing to pay your bills.

## Diversify your assets

One of the most common methods of managing investment risks is to diversify.

You've probably heard the cliche: Don't put your eggs all in one basket. Because if you do, and something happens to that one basket, you'll potentially lose all your eggs.

Diversifying means investing in different types of investments (stocks, bonds, real estate, currency, cash, mutual funds, annuities, life insurance, etc.).

It also means investing in different types of securities within an investment class. For example, if your retirement plan is 75 percent invested in stock mutual funds, you will want to diversify that 75 percent among different sectors, such as large companies, small companies, foreign companies, energy companies, and financial companies, as an example.

The lower your risk tolerance, the more diversified you should be. Spreading out your assets lowers the chances of losing a large share of your overall portfolio at any one time. It does, however, mean your potential returns will be lower than if you concentrated your investable assets on fewer options.

## Hedge your investments

Hedging an investment minimizes its potential loss if its overall value falls. This is done by purchasing an option, which gives you the right to sell your asset at an agreed-upon price if its value begins to dip. Because it minimizes risk, hedging also reduces your potential return.

## Take a long-term approach

If you've ever followed movements of the stock market or a particular stock, you know that values can ebb and flow. But over time, chances are your investment will increase in value over what you initially invested. The longer your time horizon, the better the odds of having gains in your portfolio instead of losses. For example, the chances of having a higher return after 25 years is greater than the chances of a higher return after just 10 years.

## Take advantage of dollar-cost averaging

A common mistake people make when investing is to stop contributing money when the market(s) they're invested in starts to fall. The thinking is that they'll lose even more money than they already have by contributing more during a declining market.

But that could be a costly mistake. You see, there's a concept called dollar-cost averaging that can help you profit from periods when the value of your investments goes down, provided you keep investment.

Dollar-cost averaging means investing a fixed amount of money into the same investment vehicle(s) on a regular basis, such as monthly or quarterly, regardless of how the market is performing.

This is how your employer-sponsored 401(k) plan works. You probably contribute the same amount from each paycheck into your retirement plan. But you can often use the same tactic with other investments.

How does this help? With dollar-cost averaging, you buy more shares of investment when the market you're investing in is lower. When the value of those shares increase, you benefit by owning more shares than you would had you decided not to buy shares when they were lower.

Say you make a regular contribution of $100 per pay period. That means you're buying $100 of investable assets. Hypothetically, assume each share you buy is $10 a share. So, for the next pay period, you'll add 10 shares of your investment to your retirement plan.

If the value of those shares increases to $20 a share, you'll only add five shares to your overall portfolio. This isn't bad, because the 10 shares you bought previously increased in value.

But what if the per-share value drops to $5. Yes, your overall portfolio is worth less. But the next pay period, your $100 contribution will buy 20 shares instead of 10. If the per-share price rises back to $10, you'll have 30 shares worth $10 each instead of just 20.

## THE RISK AND REWARD OF CASH VALUE LIFE INSURANCE

Cash value life insurance is also an asset that can help you meet investment objectives while managing your financial risk.

Until you started reading this book, you may not have considered life insurance an "investment." Or you might have heard financial advisors telling you to never use life insurance as an investment.

But cash value life insurance has many of the traits as your retirement plan and other parts of your investment portfolio.

Like a traditional investment, cash value life insurance includes an interest-generating account. How much interest it generates will vary based in part on the type of policy you own. Some life insurance companies also pay dividends to whole life policy owners based on the company's financial performance.

Like some traditional investments, there are unique tax rules for cash value life insurance. Life insurance death benefits are tax-free when paid to the policy's beneficiaries. Because cash value is what supports that death benefit, withdrawals and loans are tax-free as well in most circumstances. Interest grows on a tax-free basis.

## TYPES OF LIFE INSURANCE WITH INVESTMENT FEATURES

As a reminder, there are two basic types of cash value life insurance: whole and universal.

Whole life insurance is meant to cover a person for their "whole life," hence the name. The policyholder pays the same level premium for as long as they own the policy. The death benefit also typically remains the same. Whole life builds cash value from the reserves that insurers set aside to ensure they can pay a death benefit.

Universal life (UL) insurance is more flexible than whole life, but also has less of a guarantee. UL premiums support the amount of coverage you elect to own, which is called the face amount. Each premium payment you make goes into the policy's account value. After the insurance company takes what it needs to cover its costs, the leftover amount is the policy's cash value, which earns interest. You can vary the amount, timing and frequency of payments as long as the policy has enough cash value to cover expenses. It's also possible over time to increase the death benefit amount.

There are three main types of universal life, which were covered in the previous chapter. These include:

- Fixed UL polices that pay a set rate of interest determined in advance by the insurer.
- Variable UL policies that allow the owner to invest premium dollars in accounts that can gain or lose value.

- Indexed UL which typically offers better returns than fixed UL but caps its potential growth rate so that you avoid market losses.

## ASSESSING THE RISKS OF CASH VALUE LIFE INSURANCE

Cash value life insurance can help you avoid or mitigate many of the risks described earlier in this chapter.

Most notably, most types of cash value life insurance will not lose their value based on the performance of the stock market or other economic factor. The one exception is investing in a variable UL policy. The other types of UL policies and whole life insurance pay either a fixed rate of interest or provide a guarantee minimum with the insurance company taking on the investment risk.

### Interest rate risk on cash value life insurance

Because interest is credited based on fixed rates, there is some interest rate risk involved with cash value life insurance. On the one hand, higher interest rates may result in higher dividends on whole life and higher interest crediting rates on the policy's cash value. Lower interest rates can have the opposite effect.

Lower interest rates can be especially problematic on universal life policies. A UL policy's death benefit is never guaranteed. It requires a certain level of cash value to pay for the insurance company's costs of insuring your life. Not having enough cash value to pay expenses could lead to policy lapse, i.e. losing your coverage. This can occur due to insufficient premium or withdrawing too much of the cash value at once.

It can also happen if the interest credited is less than what was projected. If you paid an amount of premium based on the projection of earning, say, 6 percent, but your policy only credits an average of 4 percent, it will eventually run short of the cash value needed to keep the coverage. If you don't make additional payments to make up the difference, you could lose your coverage.

**Liquidity risk on cash value life insurance**

The liquidity benefits of cash value life insurance are a mixed bag.

On the one hand, life insurance is fairly liquid, in that you can access a good chunk of the cash value and have that money in a fairly short amount of time. You can use these funds for any purpose; there are no restrictions on their use. You have the option of not repaying withdrawals, though taking advantage of that feature will lower the policy's death benefit. Plus, as noted several times, the money is almost always tax-free.

Unlike retirement plans like 401(k)s and IRAs, there are no annual contributions limits dictated by the IRS on life insurance. IRS limits placed on life insurance are on a case-by-case basis because they are determined by how much insurance coverage you want and how much the insurance company will charge for it. It is possible to contribute $40,000, $50,000, or even more per year to a life insurance policy; the insurance company will adjust the policy to pay out a higher death benefit to avoid violating IRS rules on the definition of life insurance. This is done to ensure that people don't overbuild tax-free cash value in a life insurance policy.

One of the liquidity downsides of life insurance is that the cash value doesn't accumulate much in the first several years of the policy. A $10,000 premium payment doesn't equate to $10,000 in cash value, especially in the policy's early years. Nearly all the paid premiums in the early policy years pay the cost of the insurance coverage, which ties up your money.

**Risk of insurance company default**

Your life insurance policy may be active for many years before it pays out the promised death benefit. In the meantime, there is a risk, in most cases very small, that the insurance company will default on its obligations.

You can increase the chances of picking the right insurance company by reviewing independent financial ratings of life insurers.

There are four agencies that grade insurance companies for their financial strength: A.M. Best, Fitch, Moody's and Standard & Poor's. Ratings are based on the agency's assessment of how well positioned the insurer is financially to meet its current and future obligations, i.e. the death benefits of its policyholders. The higher a company's rating, the less risk in doing business with that company, at least from a financial strength standpoint.

## Other potential downsides of life insurance as an investment

One thing to keep in mind is that cash value life insurance costs considerably more than term life insurance. Although term policies offer no cash value, many experts suggest you invest in other conservative, low-risk investments instead of spending extra money on cash value life insurance.

Cash value life insurance also has more fees and charges than other types of investments, including:

- **Sales charges.** These cover the sales expenses, including the selling agent's commissions.
- **Administration fees.** Insurance companies deduct fees from your policy cash value once a month to cover its ongoing operations, such as accounting and record keeping.
- **Mortality and expense risk charges.** Insurance companies use data and algorithms to project how long you will live. The monthly mortality and expense risk charges basically compensate the company if you don't live to that assumed age.
- **Cost of insurance.** This is what the insurance company charges to provide coverage on your life. The amount is based mostly on your underwriting criteria, including age, gender, health and the amount of coverage.

Also, as mentioned throughout this book, withdrawing cash value from your policy will reduce its death benefit until you repay the loan. If you don't repay the loan before you pass away, the policy's beneficiaries will not receive as much of a death benefit.

## HOW YOU CAN USE LIFE INSURANCE

Because of its flexibility and tax-free status, life insurance offers a versatile way to meet a number of financial objectives.

Many people are using cash value life insurance to supplement their retirement income. It's one of the few ways to can save for retirement that essentially guarantees you will never lose principal, while also providing flexibility and overall control of your money.

Like with other types of retirement investments, it's important to start as young as possible. This provides time for a life insurance policy's cash value to grow enough to fund retirement income when it's needed.

When it comes time to begin withdrawing retirement income from your policy, you can benefit from:

**Flexible cash withdrawals.** Unlike with 401(k)s and other retirement accounts, you can withdraw money before you reach age 59 1/2. You also are not required to take required minimum distributions (RMDs) starting at age 70. There is never a tax penalty with life insurance for withdrawing money too soon or waiting too long.

**Tax-free cash value withdrawals and loans**. You can borrow up to a certain percentage of the your policy's cash value, typically about 90 percent. Perhaps the best advantage of life insurance loans is that the money you borrow will earn interest even while you're repaying it. These loaned funds are typically tax-free income. Plus, you are not required to pay the loan back, though not paying back the full loan amount will typically be deducted from the death benefit. However, many people who reach retirement age no longer have as many dependents who would need life insurance proceeds.

In addition to retirement, one of the most popular uses for cash value life insurance is to help fund a child's or grandchild's college education. If you start saving money in a policy soon enough, you can accumulate cash value to help with a portion of those college expenses. What's more, life insurance doesn't have the same restrictions as 529 college savings plans. Plus, life insurance doesn't impact the financial aid your child or grand-child could qualify for because it's not considered income or a financial asset.

The cash value inside your policy can be used for anything you would normally go to a bank to finance: new car, home remodel, or a business expansion. You don't have to apply for a loan, which means no paperwork, no credit checks and no rejections. What's more, using your policy will potentially save you thousands of dollars in interest payments.You'll probably save even more in interest payments using life insurance instead of a credit card for major purchases.

**Chapter 5 summary**

There are risks in nearly every aspect of our lives. This is especially true in the realm of money and investments.

In this chapter, you learned about the risks most associated with investing, plus how to measure and minimize those risks.

This chapter also explored how cash value life insurance, such as whole life and universal life, can be both a protective measure and investment tool. I also outlined the key risks and benefits of policies with investment features like tax-free withdrawals and cash value loans.

Chapter 6 will include a deeper dive into the types of life insurance to choose from and tips on how to make an informed decision based on your individual financial goals and needs.

# EVALUATING LIFE INSURANCE POLICIES: MAKING THE RIGHT CHOICE

*"Savings alone are not enough to achieve financial freedom; insuring your assets with general insurance policies is equally important."*

— IFFCO-TOKIO

This chapter will cover a lot of the nuts and bolts of buying life insurance: what to buy, where to buy it, how much to buy and a number of other details.

To begin, I'll cover one of the most important distinctions to consider when buying life insurance: the difference between term life and permanent life.

## TERM LIFE INSURANCE

Term life insurance pays a death benefit only if the covered person dies during a specified period.

That period begins on the date the policy is issued. The coverage remains active until the end of the term, as long as you pay your premium. If you buy a 20-year term, your life insurance coverage terminates 20 years from the issue date if you don't pass away.

When a term policy expires, you have to renew your life insurance if you want to stay covered. Your new policy, assuming it's for the same amount of coverage, will cost more than the original policy.

Term life insurance is an affordable way to provide cash to replace your income if you die. It helps survivors pay bills, cover debts, and pay for funeral expenses.

There are a number of types of term life insurance; here are the most common:

**Level term life insurance**

Level term is popular and gets its name because neither the death benefit nor the premium amount change during the policy's term period.

Level term comes in many increments, with the most common being 10, 20 and 30 years. Longer term periods cost more because the chances of having to pay a death benefit increase for the life insurance company the longer you are covered.

## Annual renewable term life insurance

Annual renewable term (ART) insures your life for one year at a time, with the option of renewing it annually. ART premiums start out lower than comparable level term policies, but increase over time.

## Increasing term life insurance

Increasing term life insurance provides a death benefit that increases over the life of the policy. It is designed to provide increasing protection to meet your growing needs. These may include:

- A single person who buys increasing coverage in anticipation of having a family later.
- Somebody who doesn't own a home but might in the future.
- Ensuring your coverage can keep pace with inflation.

The death benefit grows in increments, such as 5 percent annually, throughout the policy term. No additional underwriting is required to increase the coverage amount, but premium payments are higher.

## Decreasing term life insurance

Decreasing term life insurance is a type of term coverage in which the death benefit decreases as an insured person ages. Premiums remain the same throughout the term period. Terms range between 1 year and 30 years.

It is a good option for people who may have less need for life insurance later in life as children get older and other financial obligations, such as a mortgage or school loans, decline. Because the death benefit decreases, this coverage costs less than level term insurance.

## Group life insurance

Group term life insurance covers several individuals who are part of the same group. It is often available through employers and professional associations. Group life insurance could be an affordable way to supplement your other life insurance coverage.

It is less expensive to buy group term than individual term. In some cases, the group that sponsors your plan, such as your employer, will cover the full cost and make it free to you. Many group policies are guaranteed issue with no underwriting requirements.

Keep in mind group policies usually limit your coverage amount. Employers, for example, may cap your benefit at an amount based on your current salary.

## Accelerated underwriting (AU) term life insurance

Accelerated underwriting allows you buy term life insurance without a medical exam. You will also not be required to give blood or urine for lab testing.

The underwriting process for an AU policy involves a short medical questionnaire. Your responses will help the insurance company determine if you qualify for coverage, or if you need to go through full underwriting.

If you qualify for accelerated underwriting you will be issued a policy sooner than if you have to go through traditional underwriting. Also, some insurance companies may limit how much coverage you can apply for using AU, especially if you have reached a certain age.

### Return of premium term life insurance

There's a rider available on many term policies called the return of premium. Adding this rider entitles you to a refund of all the premiums you paid if you outlive the term and it expires without paying a death benefit. Some insurers automatically include this feature on term policies.

The rider may increase your premium amount, but you'll receive some of it back if the insurance never gets used.

### Term life insurance cost

According to NerdWallet, the average cost of term life insurance as of September 2023 is $26 a month. This is based on a 40-year-old buying a 20-year, $500,000 term life policy, which the site wrote is the most common term length and amount sold. Using the site's calculator, other rates for term life insurance included:

- Depending on health, a 30-year-old female can get a 30-year, $500,000 term policy between $25 and $41 a month. The same policy for $750,000 in coverage would run between $35 and $59.

- A 30-year-old male can get a 30-year, $1 million policy for between $52 and $88 a month.
- Depending on health, a 50-year old female can get a 30-year, $500,000 term policy between $95 and $144 a month. The same policy for a man would run between $123 and $200 a month. A 20-year policy would run between $69 and $113 for a male and between $55 and $84 for a male.
- A 65-year-old female could buy a 10-year, $300,000 policy for between $77 and $121 a month. A man could buy the same policy for between $113 and $171.

Many variables affect the cost of term life insurance, including:

- **Age**. Older individuals pay more.
- **Gender.** Men are typically charged more for having a lower life expectancy.
- **Your coverage amount.**
- **Term length.** The longer the term period, the higher the cost.
- **Additional features you add.** Many riders require additional premium above what the standard coverage costs.
- **Your health**. The cost of term life insurance is mostly based on the likelihood that the insured will die during the term period. Therefore the healthier you are, the less you will pay. If you use tobacco or have certain chronic conditions, you will likely pay more than if you were in perfect health.

- **Lifestyle**. In addition to health, insurers often assess your risk based on your lifestyle. If you have a dangerous or stressful job, for example, it may negatively impact your premium cost. Frequent international travel and dangerous hobbies such as skydiving can also affect your rates.

**Term life insurance pros**

The benefits of term life insurance include:

- **The cost**. Term life insurance is far less expensive than permanent life insurance. In fact, buying the same amount of whole life insurance can cost between four times and nine times more. The shorter the term you opt for, the more affordable the premium.
- **Frees up funds for other goals**. By not spending as much on life insurance, you can budget more of your income to other life goals, such as saving for a house, college, or retirement.
- **Coverage only when you need it most**. Many people don't need life insurance for their entire life. They may only need it primarily during the years they have children living at home. Term insurance enables you to only pay for coverage for as long as your protection needs exist.
- **Straightforward and generally easier to understand**. Term life insurance is a much simpler product than permanent coverage, especially if you opt for level term coverage.

- **Usually tax-free**. The death benefit the policy pays out is not considered taxable income. Therefore if a benefit is paid out, your beneficiaries will not owe taxes on the amount, not matter how much it is.

**Term life insurance cons**

Despite its simplicity and affordability, there are a few downsides to buying term life insurance:

- **Coverage only lasts for a certain amount of time.** Term insurance is temporary. If you buy a 20-year policy, your coverage expires after 20 years. There's a good chance you'll pay premium for several years and receive no benefits in return.
- **Level rates will end**. If you decide to renew your term policy after it expires, you will be paying much higher premiums. That's because you will have to go through underwriting. You'll be older and your health may not be as strong as it was when you purchased coverage at a younger age.
- **No cash value**. Term life insurance does not accumulate cash value for you to access as many permanent policies do.

## WHEN SHOULD I CONSIDER TERM LIFE INSURANCE?

Term life insurance is typically the best coverage option for people who:

**Want or need the most affordable coverage.** Term is for those who can't afford permanent coverage or who would rather spend less of their income on life insurance.

**Will retire with enough savings to self-insure.** This means you will have enough in savings to cover the loss of income caused by the loss of the life of a wage earner. If this is the case, a term policy can supplement that savings or cover one-time expenses like funeral costs and settling the deceased's estate.

**Don't plan to financially support adult children.** Once you're no longer financially responsible for children, you have much less need for life insurance. Therefore, you don't necessarily need a permanent policy. You can buy a term policy that lasts up until your children are on their own.

**Have outstanding debts or a mortgage.** If this is the primary reason for buying life insurance, then the need diminishes as you pay off those debts. For example, if you get a 30-year mortgage, you can theoretically buy a 30-year term policy that expires when your mortgage is scheduled to be paid off.

PERMANENT LIFE INSURANCE

As covered in previous chapters, there are life insurance policies you can buy once and keep your entire life. Your coverage remains active as long as premiums are paid in full and on time.

As a reminder, the types of permanent life insurance are:

- Whole life, which provides a lifetime death benefit that never changes for a premium amount that never changes.
- Universal life insurance, which is more flexible, but also more expensive and more complicated than whole life. It comes in three types: fixed, variable and indexed.
- Burial/final expense life insurance, which provides a small death benefit for the purpose of covering funeral expenses and other costs that arise when a person dies.
- Survivorship life insurance, which covers two lives under a single policy and is often used in estate planning strategies.

**Permanent life insurance cost**

As previously stated, permanent life insurance is going to cost much more than comparable term insurance. One similarity is that both types of insurance base rates on roughly the same underwriting criteria.

According to Forbes Advisor research done in March 2023, these are the average annual rates for $250,000 in whole life coverage:

- Female, age 30: $2,219
- Female, age 40: $3,296
- Female, age 50: $4,837
- Male, age 30: $2,536
- Male, age 40: $3,639
- Male, age 50: $5,220

These are the average annual premiums for $250,000 in universal life coverage:

- Female, age 30: $1,157
- Female, age 40: $1,679
- Female, age 50: $2,456
- Male, age 30: $1,254
- Male, age 40: $1,814
- Male, age 50: $2,663

The website Policygenius researched sample premiums in June 2023 and listed the following costs for a 55-year-old male non-smoker with a preferred health rating:

- A $250,000 whole life policy cost $692 a month
- A $25,000 guaranteed issue policy cost $168.49 a month
- A $25,000 simplified issue policy cost $85.06 a month

### Permanent life insurance pros and cons

With permanent life insurance, you have the benefit of lifetime coverage, as long as you continue to pay the required premiums.

The other key benefit of permanent life insurance is the cash value component. Over time, you can use the cash value of a permanent life insurance policy as a savings account from which you can access funds for a variety of purposes, typically on a tax-free basis.

Permanent life insurance also provides more optional and flexible benefits than term life insurance. Plus, like term life, the policy's death benefit is not taxable income to your beneficiaries.

On the downside, because permanent life insurance does not expire, it is far more expensive than term life insurance. Insurance companies have to charge more for a policy that is more likely to pay out a death benefit than a term policy that has an expiration.

The higher cost of permanent life insurance makes it more likely for owners to lapse the policy. This happens if sufficient premiums are not paid to keep the death benefit in force. Policy lapse is even more of a risk on universal life policies because interest rates may fall short of what was projected, which means the cash value won't be enough to cover the insurance company's fees for providing coverage.

Despite the presence of cash value, permanent life insurance can lead to liquidity risk. First, permanent life insurance policies have surrender charges. These are penalties incurred if you decide to cancel your policy within a certain number of years after purchase. Another type of liquidity risk occurs when you withdraw funds from the policy's cash value; the policy's death benefit is reduced by the amount you withdraw.

As explained in a previous chapter, your cash value accumulation will be small in the policy's first years because the insurance company is using most or all of your premium to cover its costs.

Permanent policies are also more complex than term insurance. This is due to the multiple layers of benefits, riders and other features. Because of this complexity, it is possible to have tax implications with the use of permanent life insurance, especially since tax laws are constantly evolving. You may need to consult a tax expert when using permanent life insurance as an investment or asset.

### When should I consider permanent life insurance?

Permanent life insurance is primarily for people whose coverage needs will likely remain for a lifetime. These include:

**People with lifelong dependents.** One example of this is a parent with a special needs child. Even as an adult, the child will need ongoing medical care and likely can't earn a living on their own. Parents should be covered by permanent life insurance to provide a death benefit that can meet the needs of that child.

**People whose estates may incur estate taxes.** If your estate is large enough today that your beneficiaries will owe estate taxes on their inheritance, that need will likely never go away. Therefore, if you want to provide a way for heirs to cover those estate taxes, you should be covered by a permanent policy that will guaranteed a lifetime death benefit.

**People who plan to use life insurance to help fund retirement**. You can't accomplish this objective with a term policy since it does not have a cash value component.

**People who just want to cover funeral expenses.** This is another example of a need that will always be there. Therefore, you should have a permanent final expense policy that offers coverage no matter how long you live, provided you pay the required premiums.

In addition to these scenarios, another example of a person who should consider permanent life insurance is one who can't get traditional coverage due to health concerns. In this case, the individual can get a guaranteed issue or maybe a simplified issue policy guaranteed to last as long as the insured lives. Although it won't provide as much as a traditional policy, guaranteed issue policies provide at least a little bit of money to cover expenses that arise when a person passes away.

## HOW MUCH LIFE INSURANCE DO I NEED?

Life insurance helps financially support the people who depend on your income by providing a cash payment in the event you pass away.

One of the hardest questions to answer is: How much life insurance do I need?

Perhaps a better question would be: How much would *they* need if I couldn't provide for them?

There are a number of formulas people use to determine an amount. Some multiply their current salary by a number. This could be anywhere from six times to 15 times.

Others suggest multiplying your current salary by the number of years you have left until your anticipated retirement. For example, if you earn $80,000 a year and you have 25 years until you plan to retire, you would purchase $2 million in coverage.

It may be best to conduct a personalized assessment of your family's current and future needs. Add up things like:

- Basic living expenses for five, 10 or 20 years
- The potential cost of college for your children
- The amount of debt that could be left if you pass away, including your mortgage
- How much you have saved
- How much you have invested in your own business

One last thing to consider is that, at the very least, you should have some life insurance. It's better than having none in the event tragedy does happen. Plus, you always have the option of buying more coverage at a later date.

## WHAT IS A LIFE INSURANCE RIDER?

Riders have been covered a little in previous chapters. Think of them the same way you would optional features on a car, electronics or vacation packages. They enhance your purchase and your experience, usually for an extra cost. You may like some of these options and think others are a waste of money.

The optional features on insurance policies are called riders. They are designed to provide an enhancement to the death benefit or add features above and beyond the death benefit.

## How do life insurance riders work?

Depending on the insurance company, some riders are included for free. Others require additional premium beyond what is needed to fund the policy's death benefit. Most riders must be elected at the time you apply for insurance. They can typically be dropped later without affecting your death benefit coverage.

As you consider what riders to add, you need to weigh the cost of those optional features with the potential benefits you or your beneficiaries may receive from those add-ons.

### *Common life insurance riders*

The following are the most common life insurance riders. These will likely be offered by most insurance companies. In addition, many of them are available on both term and permanent policies.

## Health-related life insurance riders

**Accelerated benefit rider**. This rider entitles the owner to receive part of the policy's death benefit before they pass away, if diagnosed with a terminal illness. It's mainly used to cover the costs of terminal illness care.

**Critical illness or chronic illness rider**. This rider entitles the owner to receive part of the policy's death benefit before they pass away if they receive a chronic or critical illness diagnosis. One insurer's definition of chronic or critical illness will differ from others. Most typically consider strokes, heart attacks and cancer as illnesses that qualify.

**Long-term care (LTC) rider.** This rider pays a monthly benefit to the insured if they must stay in a nursing home or other long-term care facility.

**Waiver of premium disability rider.** Having a disability makes it difficult to work and earn an income. That makes it a challenge to keep up with your life insurance premiums. This rider will put your premium obligations on hold if you suffer a disability that affects your ability to earn a living. Even though you're not paying premium, your life insurance coverage remains in tact if you have and exercise this rider.

**Family-related life insurance riders**

**Additional insured rider.** You can add a rider that covers a second person. Use it for your spouse or business partner.

**Child rider**. You can also add a rider to provide death benefit coverage for your children, natural or legally adopted. Most people forgo separate life insurance coverage on children, because a child's death is unlikely and the financial loss would be minimal if it did occur. A small amount of coverage, however, can help cover funeral and other expenses that would result if the worst happened.

**Family income rider**. A family income rider is an optional add-on that, if you pass away, will pay out the policy's death benefit in monthly installments instead of a lump sum.

## Other common life insurance riders

**Accidental death and dismemberment (AD&D) rider.** Also known as a double indemnity benefit, AD&D coverage provides a larger death benefit, often double the amount you bought, if you die from an accident. Keep in mind that insurance companies often have different definitions for "accidental" death. The insured's death has to meet the policy's definition in order for it to pay out the higher benefit.

**Cost-of-living rider**. A cost-of-living rider allows your policy to increase in value over time to keep pace with inflation. This potentially provides your beneficiaries with a larger death benefit. Depending on how the rider is structured, it may increase the policy's death benefit incrementally, such as every five years. Insurance companies often place a cap on how much the death benefit can increase over the life of the policy.

**Guaranteed insurability rider**. This rider allows you to start with a lower death benefit and increase it over time. Plus, this added coverage comes without the hassle of more underwriting or a new application process. It's automatic if you elect to exercise the option. Some insurers call it a Guaranteed Purchase Option rider. It works differently with different insurers. Some let you increase your benefit at intervals, such as every five years. Other versions of the rider give you the option to up your coverage when you reach certain ages. You can often add coverage with the rider following the birth of a child or other major life event.

**Return of premium rider**. As covered in the previous chapter, this rider refunds all the premiums you paid if you outlive the term and it expires without paying a death benefit.

**Term life insurance rider**. This is a rider found on permanent policies. It adds term life coverage to your permanent policy. It's a way of making your policy more affordable by blending the two types of coverage, or by affordably adding coverage above and beyond the permanent policy death benefit. Keep in mind the premium that pays for the term rider does not get added to the permanent policy's cash value. At any point, you can convert the term rider into the permanent coverage.

**Term conversion rider**. This benefit gives you the option of upgrading an existing term insurance policy to whole life or universal life. You can make this conversion without having to go through underwriting; the underwriting used to buy your term policy will be used in the new permanent policy.

## CHOOSING THE RIGHT LIFE INSURANCE POLICY

Here is a step-by-step guide to buying the best coverage for your individual needs:

**Step 1: Understand your options**

The initial step to take when purchasing life insurance is to understand your options. You can buy term or permanent insurance. You have several options for term policies and a few different permanent insurance policies. You can buy a larger policy with full underwriting that will replace your income for many years to come, or you can opt for a smaller, guaranteed issue policy to cover a few final expenses when you pass away. Also take into account that you can add riders to enhance your coverage, whether you opt for term or permanent insurance.

**Step 2: Enlist professional help if you need it**

Because of the complexity of buying life insurance, you may want to enlist the assistance of a licensed insurance professional. If not, there are other ways to buy life insurance without using an advisor.

Independent agents or brokers are professional advisors or organizations that are not affiliated with a specific insurance company. They can offer policies from multiple companies. The advantage of this is that they can help you compare rates and features on several options and get you the best deal.

Affiliated agents, also known as captive agents, typically sell one or a few company's products. You won't receive as many options with an affiliated agent, but the professional you work with will likely have more familiarity with the policies they sell than an independent who works with multiple insurers.

Whether you work with an independent or affiliated professional, you should know that in most cases the person you work with earns a commission from the insurance company. This commission is largely based on the amount of coverage you buy and how much premium you will pay. Therefore, they will also earn more commission selling a permanent policy than they will a term policy.

Working with an agent is advantageous in that they can handle a lot of the paperwork. They can also help you determine the right amount of coverage. Oftentimes they will advocate on your behalf to get a better underwriting outcome. They can also contact the insurance company on your behalf if there are any questions about your coverage. Plus, they can help your beneficiaries file a claim for the death benefit, if needed.

If you don't want to work with an insurance professional, you can often buy direct from an insurance company, typically on their website.

If you're looking for group coverage, you can buy through your employer or an organization that you are a member of, such as a trade organization.

**Step 3: Determine your coverage needs**

Your life insurance coverage amount should provide for the long-term needs for whoever you designate as the policy's beneficiary. There are a number of calculators and formulas you can use to determine a proper amount (see earlier section of this chapter: How much life insurance do I need?). You can also work with a licensed insurance professional to assess your coverage needs.

**Step 4: Determine your budget**

Life insurance will be a long-term expenditure. You should determine what you can spend. This will help you determine the type of policy you can buy, how much coverage you can apply for, and whether you can add riders to your policy.

**Step 5: Shop around**

You can shop for life insurance from a number of carriers, comparing cost and features. Avoid limiting your search to one policy or recommendation, and obtain quotes from multiple insurers.

Keep in mind the cheapest policy may not always be your best option. Look over contract provisions, optional riders and under-writing standards. One insurer may consider you a higher risk than another because of their internal underwriting guidelines.

Comparison shopping should also include examining each prospect's financial ratings (See Chapter 5; Risk of insurance company default). Most companies post their current financial ratings on their websites or in their annual reports.

**Step 6: Complete the application process**

Once you've landed on what to buy and where to buy it from, the next step is applying for coverage. If you enlist the help of an agent, they can help you fill out the form, which will likely be several pages.

Unless you're buying guaranteed issue, be prepared to answer several health related questions. This includes whether you have used tobacco, conditions you have been diagnosed with, medications you are on, and family health history. Insurance companies also ask about your job, your lifestyle, your habits, and your hobbies. These are meant to assess the risk of you dying from certain illnesses or physical injuries.

You will also likely have to provide supporting documents, including proof of identity, age, and citizenship. Because insurance companies are regulated at the state level, you will need to prove you're a resident of the state from which you're buying the policy. You will also have to provide documents that prove your current income. Authorizing release of medical records to the insurer is also part of the process.

The application will ask you to designate beneficiaries. This is the person or people who will receive the death benefit if you pass away. This will typically be a spouse and/or children. You can also name a trust that will be designated to hold the money meant for minor children until they become adults.

It's extremely important to answer all application questions honestly. If the insurer discovers you obtained coverage based on false underwriting information, it may take one of two actions.

You may receive a lesser death benefit based on the amount of coverage you would have received had the insurer knew the truth. If the discrepancy was egregious or outright fraudulent, the insurance company can deny a death benefit claim and refund premiums paid.

**Understanding when an insurance company can contest a claim.** Something that works in the applicant's favor is that insurance companies can only contest a claim if it's made within a certain number of years from when the policy is issued. This is called the contestability period.

Insurance companies can contest the information you submitted on your application in the first two years after the policy is issued. If they find inaccurate or misleading information, they have cause to potentially deny any death benefit claim made during the contestability period.

But if the insurance company investigates and finds no wrongdoing, then it must pay your contractual death benefit.

Insurance companies typically cannot contest a claim if your death falls outside the contestability period.

### Step 7: Get Your Medical Exam

Upon receiving your application, the next step is to schedule a medical exam, which the insurance company will arrange, unless you applied for a guaranteed issue or simplified issue policy.

The exam gives the insurance company more accurate information about your current health. Sometimes the exam uncovers medical conditions even the applicant wasn't aware of.

The 20-to-30-minute exam can often be done in your home.

The examiner will:

- Measure and weigh you
- Measure your blood pressure and pulse
- Take blood work to check for cholesterol, glucose, protein and HIV

- Take a urine sample to check certain levels as well as possible drug use
- Ask a series of medical questions, many of which you answered on the application. These include known health conditions; your current medications with dosage amounts and frequency; hospitalizations and procedures you've had; family medical history; and lifestyle choices such as diet, exercise and alcohol and tobacco use.

## Step 8: Await Underwriting Results

Once the insurance company has all the information it needs, it will complete its underwriting process to determine your insurability and, if applicable, how much it will cost to provide you coverage. Depending on the company, this could take a few months.

If you qualify, the insurance company will provide an offer of coverage. This offer may be the same, more or less than what you applied for. Any difference will likely be the result of your medical exam and other underwriting criteria.

For example, the examiner may have noted that your blood pressure was high. This may adversely affect the premium rate you expected to pay.

Keep in mind you do not have to accept the company's offer. You have the option of applying at a different company. Also, if you think you can get better results from the medical exam, you can try applying a few months later if you want to try losing a few pounds or lowering your blood pressure or cholesterol level.

**Step 9: Get Your Policy**

A life insurance policy is a contract. You agree to pay a certain amount of premium. The life insurance company agrees to provide the coverage stated in the policy.

Once you sign and return the policy, you're essentially agreeing to the terms of the contract. Therefore, before you do that, make sure you read and understand what's in it, including the fine print. Know the coverage limitations, the exclusions, late fees, what happens if you miss payments and anything else that could affect your coverage. If you enlisted an agent, have them explain anything to you that doesn't make sense.

Your coverage is active as soon as you make your first premium payment. You need to make required payments on time to keep the policy active and your beneficiaries protected.

**Don't forget that your policy will have a free-look period**. Once your policy is issued and delivered to you, the free-look period starts.

The free-look period is a time period after the policy is issued in which you can legally cancel the contract without penalty and receive a full refund of premiums you paid up to that point. Each state's insurance regulations provide a minimum of 10 to 30 days after policy delivery. Some insurers' guidelines offer more time than what certain states require.

**Store your policy and review it regularly.** Finally, make sure you store the policy in a secure place. Also, make sure your beneficiaries know about the policy and where they can find it. If they don't know it exists, they won't know to look for it so that they can file a claim if you die. And if you die, you won't be around to tell them where to find the information.

You should also review your policy at least once a year to ensure it still meets you needs. Changes in your life may necessitate more coverage. In addition, you may want to change or add beneficiaries due to changes in your family.

## Chapter 6 summary

This chapter provided a comprehensive analysis of life insurance policies, comparing term and permanent options, exploring various policy features and riders, and guiding you through a step-by-step process to choose the most suitable life insurance policy for your specific circumstances.

Now that you understand the basics of life insurance, it's time to dive into advanced life insurance strategies. In the next chapter, I'll cover how to use life insurance as a tool for building tax-free financial wealth, maximizing retirement income, optimizing estate planning, and achieving long-term financial success.

# ENHANCING YOUR FINANCIAL PLAN: ADVANCED LIFE INSURANCE STRATEGIES

*"You don't buy life insurance because you are going to die, but because those you love are going to live."*

— ANONYMOUS

One of the major points I want to get across in this book is that life insurance is more than just insurance. It is a versatile, valuable financial tool.

In this chapter, I'll cover three financial planning strategies utilizing different types of life insurance. These strategies demonstrate how there is almost always a solution to your financial needs using life insurance. By the end of this chapter you will learn:

- How to save money by buying three or more life insurance policies instead of just one.
- How to use permanent life insurance to supplement your retirement income on a tax-advantaged basis.
- How life insurance used in conjunction with other planning tools can help you efficiently and fairly transfer your assets upon your death.

## HOW TO MAXIMIZE LIFE INSURANCE WITH THE LADDER STRATEGY

For many people, the need for life insurance diminishes as you get older and have fewer dependents and obligations. But it may not go away completely.

This creates a dilemma:

- Buy a larger policy for a longer term that covers the needs for the early years, but becomes a larger expense than you need in later years.
- Buy a short-term policy that covers the needs for the early years, then hope you can qualify for affordable coverage for what your needs will be in later years.

Fortunately, there's a third, more cost-efficient option: The Ladder Strategy.

Laddering term life insurance involves buying multiple policies with varying term period lengths.

A common method of laddering policies is to buy a 10-year term, a 20-year term and a 30-year term with the same death benefit. It might look like this:

- A 10-year term policy for $250,000
- A 20-year term policy for $250,000
- A 30-year term policy for $250,000

In this scenario, if you unexpectedly pass away in the first 10 years, you would collect on all three policies and provide a death benefit of $750,000. If you died after the 10th year but before the 20th year, your beneficiaries would collect on the longer two policies, totaling $500,000. Between the 20th and 30th years, beneficiaries would receive the $250,000 benefit on the 30-year term policy.

You don't have to use the same death benefit amount for the three policies. For example, say you anticipate needing $1 million in coverage for the first 10 years, but only $500,000 after those early years. You could opt for a $500,000 10-year term policy laddered with a $300,000 20-year policy and a $200,000 30-year policy.

**Why you might consider a ladder strategy**

This is a potentially useful strategy for young parents.

Losing an income in the early years means the other parent would have to cover living expenses, including the mortgage. They would also be concerned with current and future education costs.

In the middle years, there may be a lower balance on the mortgage to repay. In addition, paid child care is typically less of a concern past the 10-year mark.

Once you get more than 20 years down the road, children are growing up, minimizing the need for living expenses. College tuition may also be less of a concern, as would a mortgage payment. In this scenario, the surviving spouse is likely concerned with day-to-day living expenses and retirement income.

**Saving money using a ladder strategy**

What's more, buying three $250,000 term policies with different term periods is less expensive than buying the one 30-year term policy for the full $750,000 in this scenario.

According to research by Forbes, using the average cost of five term quotes for a 40-year-old male non-smoker, buying a a single 30-year term policy for $750,000 would cost $69 a month for 30 years.

In the laddering scenario, the three $250,000 policies would cost $63 a month. After 10 years, your monthly premium for two policies would be $49 a month. The total for the remaining 30-year policy after 20 years would be $30 a month, more than half of what you would be paying for $750,000 of coverage you may not need in 20 to 30 years.

Policygenuis says you could save more if you opt for the aforementioned $1 million laddering strategy with different amounts. Its research shows the $500,000 10-year policy, the $300,000 20-year term and the $200,000 30-year policy would cost about $51 a month, while the straight $1 million 30-year policy would run about $76 a month. The lifetime savings over 30 years would be close to $13,800.

## Considerations for using a ladder strategy

The challenge of using a ladder strategy is defining your future needs and making the assumption those coverage needs will be lower.

One way to combat that is to tack on a guaranteed purchase option rider to the 30-year policy. As you read about in chapter 6, a guaranteed purchase option or guaranteed insurability rider enables you to increase your coverage after your policy has been issued without having to go through underwriting. If you see your needs increasing a few years into the laddering strategy, just exercise the rider to boost the death benefit on the 30-year policy.

It's also not a bad idea to consider a few other riders and options on the 30-year policy.

One would be a term conversion feature, which would enable you to turn that 30-year policy into permanent insurance, without going through underwriting, if you decide to extend your coverage for the remainder of your life or want to build cash value.

Other riders to consider would be those that help with serious health care issues, that were also covered in the previous chapter. These include the critical illness, terminal illness, waiver of premium and long-term care riders.

You will want to consider whether the cost savings in premium are worth the risk that you could short yourself on life insurance coverage in later years.

If you consider a ladder strategy, it's important to assess your current and future life insurance needs. Think about your income, obligations and how much your beneficiaries will need to replace your income for a given amount of time. Also consider your current budget for life insurance.

Because of the complexity involved, it is advised that you work with a qualified, licensed insurance professional to help you execute this strategy.

## LEVERAGING LIFE INSURANCE FOR MAXIMUM RETIREMENT INCOME

Another strategy that demonstrates the wealth building potential of life insurance is using permanent coverage to maximize your retirement income. This strategy also demonstrates how life insurance can be very useful to you while you're still alive instead of just being a benefit to those who survive you.

## WHAT IS A LIFE INSURANCE RETIREMENT PLAN (LIRP)?

A Life Insurance Retirement Plan (LIRP) isn't a special or unique type of life insurance or retirement plan. It's a general term related to the strategy of using cash value life insurance to supplement retirement income.

Just about any whole life or universal life insurance policy that accumulates cash value can be used to provide retirement income.

**What is the cash value?**

On permanent life insurance policies, premium payments fund the cost of insuring your life. Whatever premium is remaining after the insurance company pays itself becomes the policy's cash value. That cash value earns interest, the rate of which will depend largely on the type of permanent policy you own.

With a whole life policy, your premium remains the same throughout the life of the contract. However, the cost of insuring your life increases over time. In the early years of the policy, it will build more cash value. This will make it possible for there to be enough cash value in the later years of the policy to fund the insurance expenses without increasing your premium payments. Whole life cash value earns interest based on a rate dictated by the insurance company.

The cash value accumulation of a universal life insurance policy is a bit more complex. When you buy a universal life insurance policy, there is a minimum amount of premium you must pay to keep the policy active. This amount is based on the face amount, or the contracted death benefit, and the cost to provide life insurance to the insured, which will be based on all the underwriting criteria (age, health, etc.).

Although the cash value is needed to support the life insurance coverage, you can withdraw or loan yourself up to a certain amount. Withdrawing a policy's cash value does lower the death benefit. If you borrow or withdraw too much, you could lapse the policy and lose your coverage altogether.

**How does a life insurance retirement plan work?**

The key to using cash value life insurance for retirement savings is to pay more than the minimum premium required. This enables you to maximize your savings potential. This is often referred to as overfunding your insurance policy.

It may sound ridiculous to overpay for something. But in this case you're also building an asset. It's similar to paying extra on your home mortgage: The more you pay, the more you reduce your principal and the more equity you create.

The more you can pay in premium on a permanent life insurance policy, the more cash value you will accumulate. The insurance company will deduct what it needs from your premium payment to pay its expenses. Whatever is left over is available to you, the policyholder. And it also earns interest.

I'm briefly going to get a little technical to explain how cash accumulation works, as it's not exactly the same as accounts designed strictly for saving money.

In life insurance, there's a term known as the net amount at risk. This is the difference between the contracted death benefit on the policy and the accrued cash value.

For example, a policy with a death benefit of $250,000 and cash value of $75,000 has a net amount of risk of $175,000.

Why is the net amount at risk important? This amount determines the cost of protection provided by the insurance company.

Consider a policy with a $100,000 death benefit. The day the policy is issued, the insurance company has $100,000 at risk. That's because if you die the day after issue, it will be required to pay the $100,000 death benefit without collecting any premium.

As the policy's cash value accumulates, it functions as a reserve account that reduces the net amount at risk. The insurance company can use this reserve account to help pay the policy death benefit, which means it has to use less of its own funds.

Take the $100,000 policy I just mentioned. If the cash value grows to $50,000, the insurance company's net amount at risk has been cut in half to only $50,000. This lowers its cost of providing insurance protection. If the cash value reaches $100,000, the insurance company essentially has nothing at risk because there's enough cash value in the policy to pay the full death benefit.

This is why cash accumulation on a permanent life policy builds up slowly in the first few years. Most of your premium in the early years is used to cover the mortality cost, which is the cost of insuring you. As the policy's earnings grow faster than the mortality cost, the cash accumulation will accelerate. If you never withdrew money from the policy, at some point, the cash value could earn enough that it could be used to pay the policy's premiums until you die.

**Three advantages that help life insurance build cash value**

Permanent life insurance offers three advantages for building up cash value to later use for retirement income.

First, it provides tax-deferred growth similar to what you receive on a 401(k) or IRA. In addition, you won't pay income tax on withdrawals in most cases with life insurance, making it similar to a Roth IRA.

The second advantage is that you receive these tax advantages without the IRS contribution limits imposed on 401(k) and IRA plans. Those retirement plans limit you to an annual maximum contribution, even if you can afford to contribute more. Permanent life insurance has no contribution limits. You're only limited by how much premium you can afford and how much life insurance coverage you plan to own.

Lastly, using permanent cash value life insurance means you never lose money in the stock market or from bad investments. The cash value inside of a whole life, indexed universal life or fixed universal life policy is insulated against the risk of market losses. The insurance company provides a guaranteed cash value account that grows according to a pre-determined formula. Because life insurance cash value won't rise and fall with the movements of the market, that money will compound and grow into supplemental retirement income.

## HOW DOES LIFE INSURANCE PROVIDE TAX-FREE INCOME

Life insurers allow you to borrow money from your policy's cash value, usually up to 90 percent of the account value depending on the insurance company. Anytime you withdraw money from your policy for any reason, it's considered a loan. Therefore, it's not taxable income; you're simply borrowing money, similar to how you can borrow from a qualified retirement plan or from the equity in your home. It's no different than obtaining a student loan, a home equity loan or a car loan; since the intention is to repay the money with interest, the IRS does not consider loaned money as income.

What's great about using a life insurance policy for a "loan" is that the company doesn't set a timeframe for repaying your policy. Plus, the loaned funds continue to earn interest credits as if they were not withdrawn.

I know what you're thinking: If I'm using my policy for retirement income, I'm not going to repay a policy loan.

This is correct, but you don't have to worry about it. Here's why.

The insurance company doesn't technically need the money back to fund your policy expenses. What companies do instead is lower your policy's death benefit based on the amount of your cumulative withdrawals. That's essentially how you're "repaying" a policy loan. Your withdrawals are reducing the policy's tax-free death benefit from what it would have totaled had you never withdrawn any of those funds.

What about your beneficiaries? If you're planning to use your life insurance policy for income, chances are you have less of a need for life insurance coverage. Retirees generally don't have dependents to worry about providing for once they pass away.

But if there is still a need for a policy benefit, you can also buy a term policy in addition to your cash value policy, either a separate policy or a term life rider on the permanent policy providing your cash value. If you're only concerned with providing enough for final expenses, then a guaranteed issue final expense policy should be sufficient.

### Tax-free income vs MECs

I have to once again touch upon a technical aspect of life insurance to explain how the tax-free aspect of it works. Otherwise, it's possible to lose that tax-free status and incur tax obligations on your policy.

When discussing cash value life insurance, you may come across the term Modified Endowment Contract (MEC).

In simple terms, a MEC is a life insurance policy that no longer carries the tax benefits that traditional life insurance has.

MECs were created in the early days of cash value life insurance. Back then, unscrupulous investors discovered you could take advantage of the tax-advantage status of life insurance by stuffing a permanent policy with lots of money and watching it grow tax-free. Not only that, but before the rules changed you could withdraw that money tax-free. Life insurance become a way to invest without tax implications.

The IRS stepped in and created formulas that limit how much a person can pay in premiums for the coverage they've elected. If you exceed the maximum limit of premium on your life insurance, your policy becomes a MEC. It's still a life insurance policy that will pay a death benefit, but as a MEC it would no longer enjoy the tax advantages of other life insurance policies.

This is important if you're planning to use life insurance as a source of retirement income or to use the cash value for other purposes.

**Once the IRS relabels your life insurance policy as a MEC, any loans and withdrawals you take from the cash value becomes taxable income that you have to report as such when you file your tax returns. This is a permanent change.**

This is different than the annual contribution limits imposed on 401(k)s and IRAs. Those limits are universal and apply to everybody.

IRS limits on life insurance premiums exist on a case-by-case basis. Essentially, two people of the same age, same underwriting status and buying the same company's policy will have different premium limits based on how much coverage they've elected. A person who owns a $2 million life insurance policy can pay more in premium by IRS rule than somebody who owns a $500,000 policy.

It's important to know both the minimum amount of premium needed to keep your policy active and the maximum amount of premium to prevent the policy from losing its tax-advantage status.

How? Working with a qualified licensed insurance professional is an important step. They can help you understand how to keep your policy properly funded.

You also need to review your policy values on a regular basis. The insurance company should provide quarterly and/or annual statements that show all the pertinent details. Many companies also provide a secure website where you can view this information on an up-to-minute basis. You may have to call the insurance company's customer service or talk to your insurance agent to explain the information.

The bottom line to using cash value life insurance as a retirement income source is this:

**You must pay well over the minimum premium required to accumulate cash value, but you must not exceed the maximum set by the IRS or else you risk losing tax favored status.**

### Life insurance vs traditional retirement accounts

A life insurance retirement plan is a good option for people who have already maximized the annual contributions to their 401(k) or IRA plan and still want to set aside more from retirement.

There are a number of advantages life insurance has on those traditional retirement accounts.

As already stated, the contribution limits can be as high as you can afford as long as the policy meets the IRS definition of life insurance.

In addition, while 401(k)s and IRAs consider withdrawals as taxable income, life insurance withdrawals are not, as long as the policy isn't labeled a MEC.

Life insurance also does not have the same restriction on when you can make withdrawals. The traditional accounts don't allow you to make withdrawals until you reach age 59 1/2; doing so incurs a tax penalty in addition to reporting the taxable income. Life insurance cash value can be withdrawn at any time.

Traditional retirement plans also require you to begin taking minimum withdrawals (called required minimum withdrawals-RMDs) at age 70 1/2, even if you don't need the money. The amount of an RMD is based on a percentage of your account value. Life insurance has no RMDs. The cash value is there is you need it, but you don't ever have to withdrawal a dime if you don't want to.

One strategy is to leave your money in your 401(k) or IRA right up until you turn age 70 1/2, using your life insurance policy before then for income. This allows the money in those accounts to continue growing until the IRS forces you to make withdrawals.

Another strategy is essentially the opposite approach: Build up the cash value inside your life insurance policy and use it if and when the money runs out from your traditional retirement accounts.

One disadvantage of life insurance compared to a 401(k) or IRA is that the latter provide a tax deduction for contributions made each year up to the IRS maximum. Life insurance premium payments are not tax deductible.

## LIFE INSURANCE AND SOCIAL SECURITY

Another advantage of using life insurance as retirement income is that it won't negatively affect taxation on your Social Security payments.

That's because life insurance policy loans are not taxable income, and therefore will not impact the formula the IRS uses to determine whether to tax your Social Security benefits.

Currently, single filers with adjusted gross income (AGI) under $25,000 and joint filers with AGI under $32,000 pay no taxes on their Social Security benefits. But if an individual filer's income is between $25,000 and $34,000, then half of their Social Security benefits may be considered taxable income. The taxable amounts are $32,000 to $44,000 for joint filers.

Make more than those levels ($34,000 for single filers and $44,000 for joint filers) and up to 85 percent of your Social Security benefits are taxable. And by the way, half of your gross Social Security benefits count toward that AGI number.

Withdrawals from a 401(k) or traditional IRA also count toward that income amount because they are considered taxable income. A life insurance policy withdrawal or loan will not.

In other words, say you're a single filer with an AGI of $15,000 before withdrawing from your 401(k). A $15,000 withdrawal from that account means you'll be paying taxes on half of your Social Security benefits for that tax year. A $20,000 withdrawal means your total AGI would be $35,000, which would result in Social Security taxes on up to 85 percent of those benefits.

Take out either size withdrawal from your life insurance policy instead, and your Social Security benefits remain tax-free.

Another way life insurance can complement Social Security income is that it can help replace the income lost when one spouse dies. Spouses will either both receive workers' benefits or one will collect workers benefits and a smaller spousal benefit. When one spouse dies, the survivor will experience a reduction in monthly benefits from the amount that both spouses collected. When this happens, the survivor can withdraw funds from a cash value life insurance policy to replace the lost Social Security income.

## USING LIFE INSURANCE IN ESTATE PLANNING

So far this chapter, we've covered a scenario for maximizing life insurance protection at a lower cost and how to use life insurance for retirement income.

I'll end the chapter on how to use life insurance to execute an estate plan that effectively and efficiently transfers your assets after your passing.

When most people think about estate planning, they limit the practice to wealthy individuals who have a team of attorneys setting up foundations, transferring business ownership and dividing up millions of dollars among surviving family members.

In reality, anybody who owns assets has an estate. The house and vehicles you own, your savings account and even your personal property are considered an estate. As such, if you're at all concerned with what happens to those assets after you pass away, you should have an estate plan, even if you're not leaving large inheritances for your children or grandchildren.

An estate plan is essentially a written plan describing your wishes for your estate upon your death. It often includes legal documents such as a will.

**Estate taxes**

There's much more to estate planning than paying taxes. In fact, most estates aren't large enough to be subject to federal or state estate taxes.

But since that's often what people think about with estate planning, we'll start there. Because if you have an estate that is not exempt from estate taxes, life insurance is almost a must-have.

Whether your estate owes a tax — and how much it has to pay — depends on the fair market value of your estate on the day of your death. As mentioned, your estate includes everything you own. Therefore, the executor of your estate, which you should have designated prior to your death, will be in charge of tallying up your assets and giving them a value. This includes, but is not limited to:

- Your home
- Other real estate you own
- Cash and anything contained in bank accounts
- Stocks and other investments
- Money in your retirement accounts
- Life insurance and annuity contracts
- Ownership shares in a business
- Personal property, such as vehicles, clothing or household furnishings
- Collectibles and other valuables, such as artwork, jewelry and antiques

As of this writing in late 2023, the federal estate tax applies to all estates valued at $12.92 million or greater at the estate owner's death. Current federal estate tax rates put in place in 2017 range from 18 percent to 40 percent. Current estate tax law is scheduled to expire in 2025. At that point, the exempt amount drops to $6.8 million and tax rates increase to between 40 percent and 45 percent. That means, unless the law is updated, more estates will be paying a higher tax rate in a few years.

In addition, 12 states and the District of Columbia assess separate estate taxes at varying levels and tax rates.

Federal and state estate taxes are paid from the assets of your estate before remaining assets can be distributed to your heirs. Your estate's executor is typically responsible for filing the applicable federal and state estate tax returns and ensuring that all taxes are paid.

What's more, the IRS typically only gives your executor nine months from the day you pass away to complete the paperwork and make the payment, though they can file for an extension. If it takes too long to pay those taxes, the IRS may impose penalties.

This is one of the reasons why it's critical to have life insurance if your estate is large enough.

Say, for example, you determine based on current tax rates and exemptions that your estate will owe $2 million in federal and state estate taxes. Had you purchased at least $2 million in life insurance coverage, the death benefit could go toward making the tax payments. Because life insurance proceeds can get paid as quickly as 30 days, the executor should not have a problem meeting the nine-month deadline.

In addition, using life insurance means the executor won't have to use part of your estate to pay the tax bill, leaving more assets for your heirs, beneficiaries and even to charitable interests.

**Separating your life insurance from your estate**

One of the first considerations in using life insurance for estate planning is to separate it from the rest of your estate.

I've written multiple times that the death benefit of life insurance is generally tax-free to your beneficiaries. This is true when discussing income taxes. Beneficiaries of life insurance generally do not have to report life insurance proceeds as taxable income.

However, life insurance it is not exempt from the estate tax.

If your estate is large enough that heirs will incur an estate tax bill, direct proceeds from life insurance are included in that total. That means the size of your estate for the purposes of determining the tax obligation will increase in size based on the total death benefit of your policy(s).

This can be detrimental to your estate plan, especially if you are counting on the life insurance proceeds to pay some or all of the estate tax bill. It can also hinder other estate planning strategies mentioned further ahead in this chapter.

There is a legal way to separate your life insurance proceeds from your estate so that the benefit is not subject to the estate tax.

**Transferring ownership of your policy**

There are a few steps you'll need to take in your planning to keep your life insurance out of your estate. The most important of these steps is to transfer ownership of your life insurance.

To properly use life insurance in estate planning, you cannot be listed as the policy's owner. In fact, no individual can own your policy. Neither can your estate. In any of those scenarios, the IRS will consider the policy under your control and will consider it a taxable asset for estate tax purposes.

Instead, your life insurance should be owned by an Irrevocable Life Insurance Trust (ILIT).

An ILIT is a legal trust created during the insured's lifetime. Its role is to own and control a life insurance policy or policies. It can also manage and distribute the proceeds that are paid out upon the insured's death, according to the insured's wishes. When setting up an ILIT, you will appoint a trustee to oversee it and ensure that it carries out your final wishes when you pass away. A trustee can be a bank executive, an attorney, or a financially responsible relative.

An ILIT serves as an intermediary. Because the ILIT owns the policy, the policy is not considered part of your estate in most cases.

The one exception to this provision is what the IRS calls the three-year rule. If you die within three years of transferring ownership of a policy to an ILIT, the IRS will still consider it part of your estate. Therefore, the death benefit will be considered an asset within your estate and will be calculated in your heirs' estate tax liabilities.

You may want to establish the ILIT immediately upon applying for life insurance. If you currently own life insurance and your estate may be subject to the estate tax, you should transfer ownership to an ILIT as soon as possible. An estate planning attorney can help you legally establish an ILIT.

In addition to minimizing estate taxes, having an ILIT own your life insurance has other benefits. One is that it protects your insurance benefits from divorce, reditors and legal action against you and your beneficiaries. It also keeps the policy out of the probate process.

Keep in mind there are potential downsides to transferring ownership to an ILIT that you will want to consider.

First, an ILIT is irrevocable. This means once the trust is created, it cannot be changed or revoked. The terms of the trust agreement are essentially permanent. This includes the beneficiaries of the life insurance policy within the trust.

A trust used for estate planning should be irrevocable so as to give up control. If the policy is in a revocable trust, it allows you to maintain some control over it. As such, the IRS will consider a policy inside a revocable trust as an asset of your estate and will subject it to estate taxes accordingly.

Second, once you transfer ownership of your life insurance, you forfeit all rights to that property. This means you cannot access its cash value for your own personal use. If you were planning to use life insurance cash value for retirement or other purpose, you should not transfer it to an ILIT.

**Other ways life insurance helps with estate planning**

There are a number of ways life insurance can help with estate planning.

**Preserving family assets.** Some estates run into the problem of owing estate taxes but not having liquidity to pay the bill. This is especially true if your estate contains a number of non-liquid assets, such as real estate, a business or farm. Instead of being forced to sell assets to cover an estate tax payment, you beneficiaries can use life insurance proceeds.

**Covering estate transfer expenses.** Life insurance can also help with other expenses beyond federal estate taxes that are related to estate transfer. These include paying debts, covering legal fees, and paying state estate taxes, as many states have lower thresholds for estate tax obligations than the federal tax code.

**Faster payouts**. In both of the above scenarios, your beneficiaries will likely receive life insurance proceeds far sooner than if they were forced to sell assets to cover these expenses. Just as a reminder, the IRS gives your executor about nine months to pay the tax bill.

**Business asset coverage**. If you own a business, there are a few ways permanent cash value life insurance can assist with estate planning. First, you can use the policy's cash value to assist the business if it runs into financial problems. In addition, life insurance can serve as collateral for a business loan.

Life insurance can also fund a business arrangement called a buy-sell agreement, which is an agreement put in place that allows surviving partners of a business to purchase the shares of the deceased partner from that person's estate. Buy-sell agreements are typically funded using life insurance, with the surviving partners named as the beneficiaries, who use the proceeds to buy out the deceased partner's share.

**Estate equalization**. Another common use of life insurance is to help divide an estate more equally. Conflicts often arise when assets are divided, especially when dealing with businesses or real estate that are not easy to split up equally. Estate equalization is also a priority for blended families. Life insurance proceeds can help even things out.

**Future preparation**. Estate plans don't just include transferring assets. They often include provisions for how to provide for loved ones after you're gone. Life insurance proceeds, usually used in conjunction with a trust arrangement, can be used to continue supporting a loved one after your death. This may include caring for aging adults, minors, or children with special needs. You can also use proceeds to continue making child support and alimony payments.

**Charitable organizations**. Some people want to include charitable contributions in their estate plan. You can name an organization(s) as a beneficiary of your life insurance.

### What types of policies can be useful in estate planning?

Because your estate plan will need to be executed at some point, experts suggest using permanent life insurance to fund the plan. Term life insurance could expire before you pass away, potentially leaving you without a funding source.

Permanent life insurance, on the other hand, is designed to provide a lifetime death benefit, provided you pay the necessary premiums. You can use whole life or universal life, depending on your budget and other financial goals you may have.

You may want to be careful about using the cash value for other purposes while you're alive, however, as you may risk depleting the policy's death benefit. This could leave your estate plan short of necessary funds.

If you're still married, another option is a survivorship policy, which I covered in a previous chapter. This is one policy that covers two lives and pays the death benefit after both insured individuals have passed away. A survivorship policy is typically less expensive than two separate, comparable policies.

Perhaps you don't have a large estate. But your estate plan should also include your wishes upon your death as well as a way to pay for funeral and burial expenses. A final expense policy can cover end-of-life expenses. If you have those costs covered, a final expense policy can also cover remaining debts, including medical bills left behind.

---

## Chapter 7 summary

This chapter offered three examples of the powerful potential of life insurance as a tool for building tax-free financial abundance and securing your future. Through strategic planning and utilization of various life insurance strategies, you can unlock unique benefits that contribute to maximizing retirement income, optimizing estate planning, and achieving long-term financial success.

In the final chapter, I'll cover current trends in life insurance that are critical for you to understand to use it as a wealth building tool, as well as tasks you need to take care of on an ongoing basis after you've purchased a policy.

8

# EMBRACING THE FUTURE: WHY REGULAR EVALUATION IS CRITICAL TO WEALTH PRESERVATION

---

*"I don't call it "Life Insurance," I call it "Love Insurance." We buy it because we want to leave a legacy for those we love."*

— FARSHAD ASL

---

If you've reached this point of the book, I assume you're interested in the idea of using life insurance to build, grow and preserve wealth.

If that's the case, the process isn't over the moment you receive your life insurance policy. In fact, the process won't ever really be done. There are a number of ongoing tasks , which I will cover in this chapter.

## STAY INFORMED ON THE INDUSTRY

If you plan to use life insurance as a wealth building and preservation tool, it means you'll likely carry coverage for most if not all of your life. Depending on your current age, that could be decades. In that time, the industry will continue to evolve and innovate. To get the most out of your life insurance assets, it's incumbent that you stay on top of what's happening in the industry.

Even today, in late 2023 as I finish this book, life insurance companies have been actively changing their products and operations to adapt to evolving technology, demographic trends, and the overall economy. Experts are also looking ahead to what the industry might resemble in the next 10 to 20 years and beyond.

Here are a few industry developments to consider:

**Simplifying the application process:** Insurance companies realize that younger generations insist on shorter, simpler processes when they buy. Many mortgage companies have already figured this out and have streamlined their processes. Insurance companies are getting in on the act as well. This means you can count on more use of smartphone apps, digital application processes and streamlined underwriting in the near future.

**The rise of Insurtech.** This refers to the use of technology in the insurance industry to enhance operations, improve efficiency, expand offerings, and generate more profit. Growing use of Insurtech in the industry is going to impact everything from how you buy insurance, to the products you can buy and the overall customer experience. Experts say Insurtech will create more flexibility and individual offerings to consumers of life insurance.

**Using more predictive analytics for underwriting**. Artificial intelligence and other technologies continue to make it easier for life insurance companies to assess the risk of applicants. This trend will only increase, as it reduces both the short-term cost of the underwriting process and the long-term cost of paying out claims. On the one hand, this could be good news for potential buyers who will have to succumb less to medical exams. On the other hand, technology may be less forgiving of certain underwriting conditions than humans.

**More direct selling by insurance carriers**. This trend is developing out of necessity. Life insurance agents are an aging group, and fewer people are getting into the business than are leaving. Eventually this will leave a shortage of qualified agents to sell policies on behalf of insurance providers. In the future, therefore, consumers may be buying more of their life insurance directly from the insurance companies. This may offer a cost savings for consumers, as insurers won't have to pay commissions to agents. On the other hand, it also leaves consumers more responsible for researching multiple options before buying instead of relying on the expertise of professional agents.

**More embedded life insurance**. Bundle is one of the biggest buzzwords in the insurance industry nowadays. This won't change anytime soon; it will likely get more pronounced.

This includes offering life insurance as an optional feature on other types of policies, which has not been tried much up to now. It's possible, for example, that individual health insurance policies may provide optional life insurance riders. Investment products could also get in on this trend.

On the flip side, life insurers are expected to augment their products and services to include things like buying policies on credit and getting personal accident insurance with your life policy. Life insurers are also providing more general financial tools such as budgeting apps and estate planning tools.

**Increasing self-service options**. Younger generations in general do not like calling or interacting with customer service departments. They prefer to fix problems on their own, so long as the companies they do business with provide the means to do so. Life insurers have already adapted to this trend and will continue to do so. This includes providing apps and personalized portals where customers can change beneficiaries, exercise rider benefits, get quotes, and file claims without interacting with a customer representative.

**The benefit of higher interest rates**. Since the 2008-2009 financial crisis, interest rates in the United States had hovered at historic lows. While low interest rates are great for borrowers, they are a detriment to people trying to earn interest on their savings. This includes those who use life insurance as a savings asset. However, in the post-pandemic world, interest rates have accelerated. That means banks are paying more in interest on savings accounts and CDs. And life insurance policies are earning more interest on their cash value. As long as rates stay at their current 2023 levels, buyers of permanent life insurance should enjoy better returns than policies that were bought in the previous 10 to 15 years.

## CONDUCT AN ANNUAL FINANCIAL REVIEW

Your life is going to change — sometimes a little and sometimes a lot. The world is going to change, too.

Therefore, the estate plan, the financial plan and the life insurance policy(s) you previously established may need to change over time.

At least once a year you should review all of your financial plans, goals and documents. This includes your life insurance coverage. You should definitely review everything following a major life change, such as:

- Change in marital status
- Adding a child to the family
- Buying or selling or home or other real estate
- Job change, including a substantial raise or promotion
- Starting, buying or selling a business
- Receiving an inheritance
- Death in the family
- A change in your health
- Becoming disabled
- Having a loved one require long-term care
- Retirement

It's best to conduct a review with your financial advisor and/or licensed insurance professional.

## LIFE INSURANCE REVIEW

When you review your life insurance coverage, take note of:

**Policy beneficiaries**. You can change your beneficiaries at any time by contacting the life insurance company. Many enable you to make the change online.

The people you wanted to collect the death benefit when you purchased the policy may not be who you want to be the beneficiaries 10 to 20 years or more later.

Anytime you add a child, you likely want to add that child as a contingent beneficiary. Contingent beneficiaries are those who will collect on the policy in the event the primary beneficiary dies before or at the same time as you.

A typical scenario names a spouse as the single primary beneficiary, with each child named as a contingent beneficiary collecting equal shares of the death benefit if the spouse isn't alive to collect.

You may also want to change beneficiaries in the event of getting married or divorced. If you divorce and forget to change your beneficiary, your ex-spouse is entitled to the death benefit. In the event of divorce, insureds will typically want to leave the benefit to their children. In that case, it's common to leave the death benefit to a trust that would hold the money for the children until they become adults.

**Whether you have enough coverage**. A number of life changes necessitate increasing your coverage. These include marriage, adding children, buying a house and earning more money.

If you believe you need more insurance, you don't necessarily need to replace your entire policy. In fact, doing so may be more costly because you'll be older and your health condition may have changed.

Instead, you may be able to add a term policy for a set number of years to supplement the policy(s) you already own.

Reviewing your policy enables you to consider whether to exercise a guaranteed purchase option for more coverage, if you included this feature when you bought the policy.

**How much cash value you've accumulated**. If you purchased a permanent life insurance policy, take note of how much cash value the policy has accumulated.

This is especially important if you're hoping to use cash value for retirement income or other purposes.

It's also important if you bought a universal life insurance policy. As explained in a previous chapter, universal life policies need a certain level of cash value to support the cost of insurance. Running low on cash value can cause the policy to lapse, which means you could lose coverage without an infusion of premium.

You can have the insurance company or your agent run what's called an in-force illustration. An illustration is a document that shows projections of how the policy has already performed and how it could perform in the future given certain scenarios.

**Do you still need riders?** While you typically can't add riders after policy issue, you can have them removed. This can lower your cost. Keep in mind that once you've removed a rider, you typically cannot add it back on later.

**The company that issued your policy**. As I noted above, the industry is going through a number of evolutionary changes, not unlike most industries operating in a fast-paced, technologically based economy such as ours.

As you're reviewing your policy(s), take note of the current condition of the insurance companies you have policies with.

The most important aspect to review is their financial stability. Check their current financial ratings and compare them with those ratings from when you bought your policy. If their ratings have been downgraded by third-party agencies, it may be a sign you should consider another company. You don't want to tie up your assets in a company that may collapse under financial pressure down the road. While there are recourses if this happens, it's better not to have to deal with those.

Keep updated on any changes in the company's ownership. Life insurance companies are like any other business in that they are often bought, sold, or divested. From year-to-year, the company that is responsible for your policy benefits may not be the same as the one you bought it from.

You should also keep track of any new product offerings that may enhance your current financial and estate plans.

## FINANCIAL AND ESTATE PLAN REVIEWS

In addition to your life insurance, you should conduct thorough reviews of plans and documents related to your overall financial and estate plans. This should entail:

**Assessing your investments and asset allocation**. With your professional advisor, you should review where you're invested and determine if you're getting adequate returns on your investments. You may want to diversify your portfolio, buy more of a certain investment or divest yourself of certain asset classes. You may be in a position to take on more risk, or you may decide to move money into less risky investments.

**Determining impact of tax law changes**. State and federal tax laws seem to change annually. At any time there may be new tax rates, tax brackets, tax deductions and other changes that can affect — either positively or negatively — your tax liabilities. You should meet with an accountant or tax advisor at least once a year to discuss your current situation.

**Reviewing your will**. Make sure the existing will you have on file matches your current wishes. If not, work with your attorney to update the document.

**Assessing your estate's value**. You should take an inventory of what you have, especially if you have added assets or if you've had good fortune with your investments. Compare your estate's value to current and future estate tax law to see how much, if any, tax payments your estate would have to pay upon your death.

**Organizing your documents and informing family members**. If you haven't done so already, you should package all your important documents in a safe place. Make sure the appropriate person knows where to find this information if something happens. The last thing your family members should have to do if you die is rummage through shoe boxes and desk drawers looking for your will, trust documents and bank account information. Keep everything together, and consider having a copy or two away from your home, such as bank deposit box or your attorney's office.

## CONSIDER ADDITIONAL INSURANCE TO PRESERVE WEALTH

Preserving our wealth is just as critical as creating it. In this world, there exists a number of circumstances that can erode wealth. The good news is that within our economy exist many ways to combat these potential circumstances.

You may not need all of these solutions. You may not even be able to afford all of them. They are suggestions you should at least consider and discuss with your financial advisor and/or insurance professional.

### Disability insurance

Your greatest asset is your ability to earn a living. That's one of the key reasons you need life insurance; to replace that income for the people who depend on it.

But what if you can't work because of an injury or illness?

That's where disability insurance comes in. In exchange for premium, an insurance company will replace some or all of your work income in the event you can't work because of an injury or illness.

This happens more than you think.

According to the Social Security Administration, if you are 20 years old today you have a 25-percent chance of being out of work for at least a year because of an injury or illness before you reach retirement age. Furthermore, about 5 percent of working Americans will experience a short-term disability annually due to illness, injury or pregnancy, according to the Council for Disability Awareness.

Most of these injuries are not caused by work itself, meaning they won't be covered by workers compensation.

Furthermore, the government doesn't help much either, if at all. If you do qualify for Social Security Disability, the amount you receive will be minuscule compared to your current income.

If you rely on your current savings to get through this period, it can erode your wealth very quickly. Therefore, I advise people to consider disability income insurance. As I advised in chapter 6, you can also get disability coverage as a rider with some life insurance policies.

**Long-term care insurance**

Another potential cost that can eat away at your wealth is long-term care.

With increased longevity comes higher chances of spending some part of your later years in a nursing home, in an assisted living facility, or being treated at home by a health aide.

According to Genworth Financial, the median monthly cost of long-term care in 2021 was as follows:

- $4,957 for homemaker services
- $5,148 for a home health aide
- $1,690 for adult day health care
- $4,500 for an assisted living facility
- $7,908 for a semi-private room in a nursing home
- $9,034 for a private room in a nursing home

Again, these are monthly costs. Per year, people shell out anywhere from $20,280 for adult day health care to $108,408 for a private room in a nursing home.

The expense is only going to get worse. Genworth says by 2041, each of the above costs will be nearly twice as expensive as they were in 2021.

One way to minimize the risk of losing your wealth to long-term care is investing in long-term care insurance. This is a policy that covers expenses for nursing homes, assisted living or home health aides if you cannot care for yourself.

According to the American Association for Long-Term Care Insurance (AALTCI), about 50 percent of people who bought a policy at age 65 will eventually use their policy benefits. Likewise, the U.S. Department of Health and Human Services says roughly 50 percent of 65-year-olds will need long-term care at some point in their remaining lives.

AALTCI research showed that the average cost for long-term care insurance for a 55-year-old male selecting $165,000 in level benefits was $950 a year in 2022. The same age female would pay $1,500. If you were to add a rider that increased your benefits 3 percent annually to keep up with inflation, the premium rate would be $2,220 for men and $3,700 for women. Women typically pay more than men for long-term care insurance because they live longer and are more likely to need long-term care services.

The good news is that there are tax-qualified long-term care policies in which your premiums are tax deductible.

As with disability coverage, there are a number of life insurance policies that offer long-term care benefits as an optional rider.

**Supplemental health insurance**

Between deductibles, co-pays, and co-insurance, traditional health insurance rarely covers 100 percent of your health care costs. The more serious your health care needs, the more out-of-pocket expenses you'll likely incur.

One analysis of Bureau of Labor Statistics showed the average American household spends $5,000 a year in out-of-pocket costs. The American Journal for Public Health reported that about two-thirds of all bankruptcies in the U.S. are largely due to medical bills.

Insurers offer a number of policies designed to supplement a household's regular health insurance. They are less expensive than a regular health insurance policy because they don't cover the initial cost of treatment. Instead, they provide funds to cover out-of-pocket costs you would have beyond what your regular health plan will cover.

Supplemental health is especially helpful when you incur a large health care bill for a serious need, such as cancer treatments or a surgical procedure.

For example, imagine you are diagnosed with cancer. Your treatments, including office visits, x-rays, blood tests and chemotherapy, end up costing $100,000. Depending on your health insurance plan, you might have 80 percent of those bills covered. Unfortunately, that leaves $20,000 you owe in out-of-pocket bills.

Supplemental health insurance would help cover that $20,000. Many supplemental policies even cover non-medical costs such as travel expenses to treatments.

There are several types of supplemental health insurance. There are general policies designed to cover co-pays, deductibles and co-insurance. You can also buy policies that pay out-of-pocket costs related to specific conditions, such as injuries from accidents, cancer, and critical illnesses. There are also hospital indemnity policies that cover the costs of being admitted to a hospital.

## Chapter 8 summary

It's important to realize wealth building is an ongoing endeavor. To paraphrase a popular saying: "With great wealth comes great responsibility." The more you accumulate, the more work and resources it takes to protect it from the many risks that exist in the world. Don't neglect this responsibility. That's not to suggest you have to review your plans and goals every day. But at least once a year be willing and prepared to assess and update — as necessary — your financial and estate plans, including your life insurance policies.

You should also stay aware of changes in the life insurance industry. By investing in life insurance, you'll be depending on one or more insurance companies to keep a promise for decades. You want to minimize the risk of trusting in a company that won't be there to pay out claims or provide retirement income when it comes time to access those benefits. Plus, it's beneficial to understand how technological and operational changes in the industry will affect your business with those firms.

## Making Life Insurance Easy for Everyone

Now that the path ahead is clear, you're eager to start including life insurance in your financial game plan... But before you go, why not take a moment to help someone else get started on this journey?

Simply by sharing your honest opinion of this book and a little about your own experience, you'll show new readers where they can find the clear and concise guidance they need to make sense of life insurance and discover how to make it work for their own life.

**LET'S HEAR FROM YOU!**
IF YOU ENJOYED THIS BOOK, PLEASE
LEAVE A REVIEW TO HELP OTHERS

Thank you so much for your support. The road ahead is an exciting one!

# CONCLUSION

For centuries, people of all incomes and demographics have depended on life insurance to ensure loved ones were provided for financially if they died at a time people depended on their income.

Life insurance still fulfills this critical need. In fact, a death benefit remains the most important aspect of life insurance.

But as I've covered in this book, life insurance can offer so much more.

It can be a savings account, an income source, an emergency fund, and an estate planning tool.

It is a tax-efficient vehicle for the accumulation AND protection of wealth.

It offers a way to minimize the financial risks that come with other investment sources.

Its unique benefits can unlock new avenues of financial prosperity.

It can do all this because today's policies are much more advanced than in the past. They have evolved to meet the complex needs of families and entrepreneurs in a complex world.

But in order for it to accomplish all this in your financial world, you have to take the necessary steps.

You need to seek out the professional guidance to find the best life insurance options.

You need to assess your current status and determine your future financial goals.

You need to conduct research into the types of life insurance and policy providers that work best for your needs.

You will need to commit to funding your life insurance policy so that it stays active and produces enough cash value to meet your goals.

You need to think about the future and how you want your estate to provide for the next generation.

You need to work through the life insurance application and underwriting processes until you have a policy issued to you.

You need to stay diligent after your policy is issued to ensure that your coverage remains relevant to your changing needs, the changing insurance industry, and the changing world around you.

But if you're willing to do all this, the rewards will be abundant.

You and your family will be protected against an infinite number of personal, financial and economic risks that can otherwise decimate a family's wealth.

You will build a significant source of liquid, accessible funds that you can use for a variety of purposes.

You'll have a key part of your portfolio insulated from the risk of market losses, yet one that generates the kind of returns to combat inflation.

And best of all, you'll have all this without the burden of handing over a large chunk of your income or your estate to tax collectors.

Start today by reviewing your portfolio and determine how to integrate life insurance into your financial and estate planning strategies.

# REFERENCES

Chery, Fritz. "Quotes About Insurance." Bible Reasons. Last modified October
28, 2023. https://biblereasons.com/insurance-quotes/